W9-DHJ-807

AMERICAN INDIAN LIVES

HEALERS

Deanne Durrett

Facts On File, Inc.

Healers

Copyright © 1997 by Deanne Durrett

Facts On File, Inc.
11 Penn Plaza
New York NY 10001

Durrett, Deanne, 1940-
  Healers / Deanne Durrett.
  p. cm. — (American Indian lives series)
  Includes bibliographical references and index.
  ISBN 0-8160-3406-0 (hc)
  1. Indians in medicine—United States—Biography. I. Title. II. Series.
R696.D87 1997
610'.8997—dc20   96-23072
[B]

Text design by Cathy Rincon
Cover design by Molly Herron
Cover photograph courtesy George Blue Spruce Jr.
Printed in the United States of America

MP FOF 10 9 8 7 6 5 4 3 2 1

This book is printed on acid-free paper.

In memory of

my father

David Martin Grantham

1918–1995

———————

CONTENTS

𓃣 🖑 𓃟

Acknowledgments   *vii*

Introduction   *ix*

TA-BOODLE
Kiowa Self-taught Surgeon (1809–1901)   1

COYOTE WOMAN, STAYS YELLOW, AND MRS. GOOD BEAR
Mandan Medicine Women (d. 1945)   12

SWIMMER
Cherokee Medicine Man (c. 1835–99)   23

CARLOS MONTEZUMA
Yavapai Apache Physician (c. 1866–1923)   34

RUTH HILLS WADSWORTH
Mescalero Apache Nurse (c. 1886–1973)   44

CHIEF TWO MOON MERIDAS
Pueblo/Blackfoot Herbalist (1888–1933)   51

HERBERT BURWELL FOWLER
Santee Sioux Psychiatrist (1919–77)   61

LORETTA SNYDER HELLE
Eskimo Physician (1930–   )   69

GEORGE BLUE SPRUCE JR.
Pueblo Dentist (1931–   )   78

LOIS FISTER STEELE
Assiniboine Physician (1939–   )   86

LORI ARVISO ALVORD
Navajo Surgeon (1958–   )   97

EVERETT RHOADES
Kiowa Professor of Medicine (1931–   )   105

Selected Bibliography and Further Reading List   115

Index   125

ACKNOWLEDGMENTS

In gathering the information for this book I have gained a deeper respect for the American Indian culture and a greater admiration of American Indian people.

I wish to express my deep appreciation to the Indian physicians who shared their valuable time and granted me interviews: Drs. Lori Alvord, Lois Steele, Loretta Helle, George Blue Spruce, and Everett Rhoades. I also thank Parker McKenzie, Ph.D, who supplied information on Ta-boodle and Kiowa history and culture; Deborah Anna Baroff at the Museum of the Great Plains in Lawton, Oklahoma, who found time, although I didn't have an appointment; and Margaret O'Pry, who helped us find the Saddle Mountain Kiowa Baptist Cemetery; Jean Waldman, a volunteer at the Red Cross who literally spent months helping me trace "Our Miss Hills," the first American Red Cross Nurse to serve overseas. And, thank you to Dorothy Cantor at the Mattatuck Museum and Thomas Fillius, Dr. Loretta R. Nugent, and Dr. Varro E. Tyler for information and pictures of Chief Two Moon.

Many others contributed to this work in many ways. I am grateful for the writings of others that I have acknowledged in the bibliographies. Additional thanks to Nicole Bowen, who gave me the opportunity to write this book, and to Emily Ross, for the encouragement to complete it.

INTRODUCTION

Before the Europeans landed on American shores, the Indians were a generally healthy people. They knew how to treat the ills and injuries common to them. No matter where they lived in this vast land, the American Indians found foods that provided a balanced diet. This sometimes included things no white person had ever tasted, such as raw liver dipped in bile and the stomach contents of young animals killed for food. European newcomers to America scoffed at the Indians drinking a beverage made from boiled pine needles—until they realized that the Indians did not suffer from scurvy. (Pine needles are rich in vitamin C, which prevents and cures scurvy.)

As the Europeans began to explore the land, they found that the native people were not one nation but many, hundreds in fact, with different languages and cultures. Despite their many differences, the American Indians of yesterday and today form a distinct group and share a respect for nature and a love for the land.

Through the ages, Indians have believed that their healers receive supernatural powers from animal spirits in the unseen world. Rituals and tribal beliefs differ from one tribe to another. Generally speaking, the traditional healer received supernatural power in a vision or dream after fasting. Sometimes these visions occurred as a result of smoking or eating hallucinogenic herbs. A vision usually consisted of an animal and objects found in nature, such as stones or feathers, along with instructions for making plant medicines and performing rituals. The spirit of a bear, buffalo, or owl, for example, seen in the vision, determined the strength of the supernatural power, or medicine. The animal believed to represent the strongest medicine varied from tribe to tribe. Strong medicine was thought to cure all ills, and the owner of a strong medicine bundle, made up of objects seen in visions, held a position of utmost respect in the tribe.

The objects revealed in visions were considered sacred. The person who saw the vision kept the sacred objects hidden in a leather medicine bag or bundled in a tanned animal skin. When called to minister to the sick, the healer performed healing rituals using the contents of the medicine bag or bundle.

Traditionally, Indian religion is reflected in all aspects of life, and the spiritual realm and healing are closely related. Healers seek the source of the illness—which may be spiritual or physical, external or internal. These tribal healers never merely treat a symptom, they attempt to cure the illness. They make their medicine from such available sources as plants, animals, and minerals found in the area. Along with ritualistic dances and songs, some healers use sleight of hand. With movements faster than the eye can see, they appear to remove a stone or some other object from the patient's body. This object is claimed to be the source of the illness. The patient's faith in the healer's supernatural powers and wisdom plays a major role in the success of the cure.

To those who maintain traditional beliefs, healing power comes in a vision, but healing knowledge is acquired through generations. Knowledge and medicine bundles are often passed from parent to child. Sometimes a child who shows promise as a healer is chosen to learn from tribal elders. The child accompanies the healer, gaining knowledge as medicinal herbs and roots are gathered. He or she watches as the healer prepares medicines for storage and makes them into concoctions and salves as needed. The medicinal portion of the plant is boiled and combined with other ingredients to form a remedy that is then given in an oral dose or rubbed on the skin. Certain plants are mixed with animal fat to make ointments or salves. Many plants are stored in the medicine bag, while others must be freshly gathered. A healer knows where to find medicinal plants and when to gather them.

Conservationist by nature, the Indians gather medicinal plants selectively, thinning a clump to ensure better growth and always leaving enough to spread or reproduce. A ritual usually accompanies the gathering of herbs and roots. The gatherer says a prayer or sings a song. Sometimes he or she leaves a bead in honor of the plant that is taken.

No one really knows how the Indians discovered which plants to use for certain illnesses. Sometimes the plant was chosen by simple logic. For example, a yellow plant might have been chosen to cure a disease that caused yellowing of the skin.

Many Indian remedies have yet to be proved useful, but a surprising number contain ingredients that are found in mainstream medicines used today. For example, willow bark, in common use among the Indians, contains salicylic acid, the same chemical compound contained in aspirin. In fact, more than two hundred indigenous plants used by Indians have been listed in the *Pharmacopeia of the United States of America* since it was first published in 1820. (The *Pharmacopeia* is the official listing of medicines and sets the standards for their use.) According to Professor Norman R. Farnsworth, an expert in natural medicines at the University of Illinois of Chicago, "About three-quarters of more than 120 drugs that are still extracted from plants for prescription pharmaceuticals worldwide were discovered following up native folklore claims."[1] This means that about ninety prescription drugs in use today contain plants once used by American Indians and other native peoples.

Some American Indian knowledge has been lost. None of the tribes had a written language until Sequoya invented the Cherokee alphabet in 1827. Soon after that, Swimmer and other Cherokee medicine men recorded their sacred formulas, permanently preserving their knowledge. The knowledge of other tribes, however, could only be accessed through the memories of the elders. Alfred Bowers and James Mooney, working for the Smithsonian Institution, studied many tribes, including the Kiowa, Cherokee, and Mandan. Tribal elders spoke to them through interpreters.

---

[1] "Herbal Healing Is Growing" *WebNews*, December 3, 1995

According to Dr. Parker McKenzie, an expert in Kiowa language, the interpreters spoke limited English and sometimes their translation was inaccurate. Few of the informants had first-hand healing knowledge. Both Bowers's and Mooney's writings are a valued record of the Indian cultures they studied, offering a glimpse of Indian healing among the Mandan and Kiowa, with an in-depth look at the Cherokee revealed in Swimmer's sacred formulas.

Traditional medicine remains a pillar of the past and a steadfast value system linking religion and healing. Modern medicine advances, each breakthrough a stepping stone to the next modern miracle. Today's Indians need the advantages of both worlds—modern surgery and pharmaceuticals, X rays and lasers, along with the religious rituals that activate faith and restore the Indian spirit. American Indian medical professionals, with the ability to merge technical knowledge and cultural understanding, are best equipped to meet the health care needs of Indians living in reservations and surrounding communities. The health care field thus offers vast opportunities to American Indians. They, in turn, have proved well suited to medical professions. Many more are needed to meet the needs of their people.

In the twelve profiles in this book, I have attempted to include different kinds of Indian healers. Some lived long ago and some practice today. Some live among their people and others travel great distances to return to their homeland periodically to teach and participate in tribal affairs. Some serve in high offices and others minister to the needs of patients on the reservation. Some practiced traditional medicine with the tools made from materials at hand and others wear surgical greens in the world of medical high technology. The medicine path merges two cultures, seeking modern advantages while protecting ancient traditions. Whether they walked the traditional path or choose the modern way, these healers all share a pride in their heritage and a loyalty to their people.

TA-BOODLE

Kiowa Self-taught Surgeon
(1809–1901)

In the late 1890s, White Horse, a once notorious Kiowa raider and war chief, became ill with a high fever and painful swelling in the area of an old war wound. Instead of summoning the medicine men to sing medicine songs and dance around his bed, White Horse called Ta-boodle to his aid. Ta-boodle, an old Kiowa warrior with a reputation as a healer, had saved many lives with his knife and bandages cut from the cottonwood tree. Ta-boodle warned White Horse that abdominal surgery would be too difficult for him to perform and extremely dangerous for White Horse. However, White Horse insisted and Ta-boodle agreed to try. White Horse braced himself. As Ta-boodle opened the lump with his knife, pus spurted from the wound. Ta-boodle allowed it to drain, then squeezed the rest of the abscess out with his fingers. He dressed the wound as he had done in many other cases, and returned to change the dressing every two or three days. Due to Ta-boodle's surgical effort, White Horse recovered and lived several more years.

Although a proven healer, Ta-boodle claimed no supernatural power, and the Kiowas did not recognize him as a medicine man. Accounts of Ta-boodle's healing techniques, however, indicate astonishing medical understanding for the place and time—Indian Territory in the nineteenth century.

At the time of Ta-boodle's birth in 1809, the Kiowa tribe had drifted east and south in their migration from the headwaters of the Yellowstone and Missouri Rivers to the southern Plains. Ta-boodle was probably born at a campsite on the Platte River several miles northeast of present-day Cheyenne, Wyoming.

Dr. Parker McKenzie, the oldest man in the Kiowa tribe in 1996, traced the details of his great-grand-uncle Ta-boodle's birth through the writings of Lewis and Clark. According to Dr. McKenzie, Ta-boodle's father was Peah-bo. The name is actually a Comanche word that refers to an unusually large mustang. Historians have translated it to mean "Big Horse." His mother was Odle-pah-yodle. James Mooney, an ethnologist with the Smithsonian Institution who studied the Kiowa Indians in the 1890s, recorded this additional information: "The father of T'ebodal [Ta-boodle] is famous for having had ten wives . . . In old times it was more common [to have many wives], in consequence of the surplus of women resulting from the killing off of the men in their constant wars." According to Dr. McKenzie, Bureau of Indian Affairs records indicate that Ta-boodle had four children and two wives. Dr. McKenzie, knowing the Kiowa sense of humor, says that "Peah-bo was just probably called 'Man with Many Wives' in jest, very likely by 'brothers' for being a womanizer . . . the name took root as a byname for him, and in the course of time, many assumed that he actually had ten wives."

The Kiowa language has eight consonantal sounds that are not represented in the English alphabet. Because of this, the language is very difficult for English-speaking people to understand. Translating Kiowa words into English is, at times, impossible. For this reason, Kiowa words appear in historical writings under various spellings and sometimes distorted meanings. For example, James Mooney in *Calendar History of the Kiowa Indians*, reported that the Kiowa name T'ebodal (Mooney's spelling of Ta-boodle) means

"One Who Carries the Meat from a Buffalo's Lower Leg." According to Dr. McKenzie, an expert on Kiowa language, Ta-boodle translates more accurately to "Calf Packer." The Kiowa used the same term for the calf of a man's leg as they used to describe the hind leg of an animal.

Ta-boodle actually acquired his name as the result of an attack by Mexican soldiers. A Kiowa war party had killed a deer. Before they finished processing their kill, the Mexican soldiers attacked. As the warriors hurriedly mounted their horses to escape, one hungry Kiowa grabbed a chunk of deer meat and quickly fastened it to his saddle. The Kiowa fled with the Mexicans in close pursuit. They rode through the hot afternoon and into the night. They stopped for a short rest, then continued on shortly before daylight. After another full day's ride, they made camp in the evening. At this time one of the warriors noticed the hind leg of the deer dangling from the young brave's saddle. After that much time in the heat, the leg had spoiled. As the young brave tossed the stinking, rotted meat into the grass, his taunting comrades began to call him *ta-boodle*, or "calf packer."

Incidents such as this often resulted in name changes among the Kiowa. Once the new name took hold the former name was forgotten.

The Kiowa, a small tribe of hunters and raiders, seldom numbered more than 1,800 while living on the open range. They hunted the buffalo, which provided food, clothing, and shelter, and gained wealth (horses for trading) by raiding enemy tribes and white settlers in Texas. According to the Kiowa, "Fighting was a man's business—that was the way he earned the respect of his people and was honored by women."[1] The Kiowa warriors, known for their fierceness, would sometimes be away on raids for as long as two years.

In the spring of 1833, soon after the tribe settled in Indian Territory (present-day Oklahoma, the Texas Panhandle, and southern Kansas and Colorado), the Kiowa warriors went west into Colorado on a raid against the Ute. They left a camp at the

---

[1] Wilbur Sturtevent Nye combined the testimony from many Kiowa to compile a first-person account of Kiowa history in his book *Bad Medicine & Good.*

mouth of Rainy Mountain Creek, a southern tributary of the Washita River in what is now southwestern Oklahoma. Ta-boodle stayed in camp with the women, children, and old men. According to an account given to James Mooney by Ta-boodle: One morning a few young men left camp to search for horses. Along the way they had a skirmish with a band of Osage (another Kiowa enemy). One Kiowa was killed and the others raced back to camp to warn of an imminent Osage attack. Almost defenseless, the Kiowas broke camp in panic and separated into four parties. Ta-boodle rode with a party that went south toward friends of the Kiowa, the Comanches. Another party, however, stopped just west of Rainy Mountain and made camp on a small tributary of Otter Creek, near the present town of Cooperton, Oklahoma. At dawn, a few days later, the Osage attacked the sleeping camp. The Kiowa chief A'date awakened and shouted to his people, "Tso batso! Tso batso!" (To the rocks! To the rocks!) A few Kiowas escaped by hiding on the rocky mountain but most were slaughtered and beheaded on the spot.

Ta-boodle may have been among the Kiowa who discovered the massacre. According to the account given James Mooney by Ta-boodle, "When the scattered Kiowa returned to look for their friends, they found the camp destroyed, the decapitated bodies lying where they had fallen, and the heads in . . . [brass] buckets as the Osage had left them."[2] This slaughter became known as the Cut Throat Massacre and the small valley where the doomed Kiowa party camped, Cut Throat Gap.

With warriors present, a later attack on the Kiowa resulted in a quite different outcome. In the summer of 1837, the Kiowa, Comanche, and Apache camped on Scott Creek, south of Fort Elliott in the Texas Panhandle. Cheyenne warriors wounded a young man as he straightened arrows, alone, outside camp. Ta-boodle joined Kiowa medicine man and leader Satank's avenging war party that killed the youth's attackers and followed their trail to the main Cheyenne war party of about fifty warriors. In the battle that followed, the Kiowa and their allies annihilated the Cheyenne

---

[2] Spoken in Kiowa and interpreted by George Hunt when Ta-boodle was about 80 years old and the oldest man in the tribe.

war party. This become known as the Cheyenne Massacre. Ta-boodle would have been about twenty-eight at the time and this may have been one of the first big battles he participated in.

As the Indians of the Plains warred against each other in the first half of the nineteenth century, white traders encroached into Indian Territory. Along with brass buckets and guns, the white men brought disease. Although these diseases took their toll among the whites, they were disastrous for the Indians, who had not been exposed to them before and had no natural resistance. Ta-boodle survived an epidemic of smallpox that spread from the northern Plains tribes all the way to the Gulf of Mexico in winter of 1839–40 and an epidemic of cholera in 1849. Those who survived, including Ta-boodle, fled to avoid exposure to the spreading diseases.

To fight these deadly diseases, the Indians used their traditional treatment, purification of the body and spirit. James Mooney wrote in his report, "The terribly fatal result of smallpox among the Indians is due largely to the fact that their only treatment for this disease . . . is the sweat bath followed by the cold plunge." The best defense against spread of the disease would have been quarantine followed by burning the victim's bedding. However, the disease spread like wildfire on the prairie and many, perhaps a third of the tribe, died in this epidemic.

The first Kiowa to become ill with cholera in 1849 died within a few hours. By that time, this deadly disease had begun to spread through the tribe. As the death toll mounted, whole families were wiped out. Some Kiowa saw the situation as hopeless and committed suicide rather than face the ravages of the cholera. Medicine men were powerless against this disease and many fell victim themselves. The loss of medicine men in this epidemic distressed the tribe further.

From the earliest remembered time, the Kiowa have placed great faith in the Doyem-k'hee, or tribal healers, whom white people called medicine men. To the Kiowa, "medicine" means "spirit power" or "mystery," not a medicinal drug. The Kiowa recognized only a select few as having the spirit power to heal. They believed that these people received this power, or medicine, from the spirits of the buffalo, water monster, or owl.

According to Kiowa tradition, Ah-tah-zone-mah, sometimes called Ah-tah, received the Buffalo Medicine in a dream when she was a young girl. This medicine became the strongest healing power known to the Kiowa. Years later, Ah-tah passed the Buffalo Medicine to her two adopted sons when they returned from their first raid. She told them of her dream and divided the contents of her medicine bag. The boys then became the first Buffalo Medicine Men. They later divided the medicine in their bags to make several medicine bags. The recipients of these medicine bags formed the Kiowa Buffalo Medicine Society. According to Old Man Humming Bird, the last surviving member of the Buffalo Medicine Society in 1937, "when members of the war party were wounded, the buffalo men would shake rattles and buffalo tails and sing their special song . . . They not only claimed great success in healing the wounded, but also became great war chiefs." Interestingly, the supernatural Buffalo Medicine only worked on wounds, not sickness.

Even with claims of great success at times, the Buffalo Medicine failed. Wounds festered and injured warriors weakened. When the Buffalo Medicine Men had exhausted their supernatural power they called upon Ta-boodle.

Ta-boodle, although not recognized as a medicine man, exhibited medical knowledge and surgical skill that in some ways exceeded that of white doctors in the 1800s. At that time, recognized treatments among white doctors consisted of purging, bleeding, and blistering. Actually poison, the purge (a dose of mercury chloride mixed with medicinal wine, laxative salts, opium, and castor oil) caused uncontrollable salivating, bleeding gums, and extreme diarrhea. These doctors further weakened their patients by bleeding them in order to eliminate the "bad blood" thought to cause illness. In order to bleed a patient, they cut several veins and drained large amounts of blood into cups. A third, not so lethal treatment involved a pasty concoction called a hot plaster spread on cloth and applied to the body. This treatment caused sweating and blistered the skin to draw fluids, thought to be poisonous, from the body. None of these treatments promoted healing but, in fact, often hastened death.

Patients who required surgery fared no better. Before doctors knew that germs caused infection and began to use antiseptics, surgery often resulted in death from infection. People soon realized that the cure was often worse than the illness. Afraid of the "heroic" surgical efforts of doctors at the time, some white people sought treatment from traditional healers, including herbalists, midwives, and Indian medicine men. They also relied on family remedies passed down through the generations.

Ta-boodle may have been among the first Indian healers to take extraordinary measures to save life. He performed surgery successfully before anyone knew about antiseptics or antibiotics. In addition, he devised a way to assure healing from the inside out in deep wounds and to stop bleeding with a primitive pressure bandage made of buffalo tallow and a small wooden cup. With no scalpel or sutures at hand, he used his sharp knife to carve his medical supplies from a nearby cottonwood tree and perform surgery as well. Kiowa oral history passed on by George Hunt bears witness to an astonishing number of his patients surviving life-threatening injuries.

George Hunt interpreted for James Mooney as a boy and grew up listening to his Uncle Iseeo and other old-time warriors, including Ta-boodle, relate the stories of their lives. As he grew older, Hunt continued to gather the history of his people. He related the stories of Ta-boodle's healing successes to Wilbur Sturtevant Nye for his book *Bad Medicine & Good*. Hunt gave no clue as to where Ta-boodle acquired his healing techniques. He, however, offered this observation: "Old T'ebodal [Ta-boodle] was not a medicine man. Nevertheless he was a clever healer and a very wise fellow." Dr. McKenzie agrees, "He [Ta-boodle] was just a practitioner who taught himself about the human body. He learned to set broken bones, doctored wounds without any occult means. He was so valuable in that regard that war parties regularly included him as a member."

Dr. McKenzie remembered hearing about a warrior Ta-boodle treated for a bullet wound to the head. In fact, a portion of the warrior's skull was blown away, exposing the brain. After cleaning the wound, Ta-boodle hammered a Mexican peso very thin and shaped it to patch the hole in the skull. He covered this with a layer of buffalo fur tied in place with strips of buckskin. The man lived to an old age and acquired the Kiowa name that translates as Metal Head.

One incident George Hunt reported occurred in the summer of 1854. The Kiowa and several other tribes fought the Sakibo Indians on the Smokey Hill River between Fort Hays and Fort Harker (Kansas), many days' travel from the Kiowa camping grounds. During the fight, a Kiowa warrior named Maunte-pah-hodal took a bullet in the buttocks. The Buffalo Society performed their ritual but the wound festered. As Maunte-pah-hodal's condition grew worse, the Buffalo Medicine Men consulted Ta-boodle. Not recognized as a medicine man, Ta-boodle faced punishment if his treatment failed and the wounded man died; nevertheless, Ta-boodle agreed to operate.

In preparation, he sharpened his long-bladed knife and asked for a brass arm band from one of the bystanders. Ta-boodle straightened and twisted the arm band to form a probe with a hook at one end. He held the knife and brass hook in a flame to purify them.

Ready for surgery, he instructed several men to place the patient buttocks-up on a pile of blankets. Ta-boodle stuffed a rag in Maunte-pah-hodal's mouth and told him to bite hard. As the other men held the patient by the arms and legs, Ta-boodle thrust his sharp knife deep into the wound until he made contact with the bullet. He withdrew the knife with a twist to open the wound further. Then he used the brass hook to dig the slug from the flesh. Infected matter oozed from the hole and Ta-boodle flushed the wound with water. When all the infection had been washed out, he filled the hole with hot buffalo tallow. He then carved a shallow cup, about 4 inches in diameter, from a piece of soft cottonwood to cover the wound. The wooden bandage not only held the edges together, but also protected the wound from flies. After the treatment, Maunte-pah-hodal's fever dropped, offering evidence that the infection had been controlled.

Unable to ride his horse, Maunte-pah-hodal made the long journey back to the Kiowa camp in Indian Territory on a travois (a platform dragged behind a horse on two poles). When the travelers made camp each night, Ta-boodle removed the cup, let the wound drain, and replaced the tallow dressing. It healed from the inside out with no further infection. By the time they reached camp, Maunte-pah-hodal could walk again.

To show his gratitude, Maunte-pah-hodal offered Ta-boodle his two sisters as wives, although one was already married. To prevent trouble, Ta-boodle accepted only the unmarried sister. According to census records, Ta-boodle and his wife, A-tong-ty, twenty-five years his junior, had five daughters and several grandchildren.

Another warrior received an even more terrible wound during a raid into Texas. A Texan shot Big Arrow in the face at close range. Fired from above, the bullet entered Big Arrow's eye socket, traveled downward knocking out teeth, leaving a hole in his throat, and finally lodging in his shoulder. The Buffalo Medicine Men came to his aid, waving their buffalo tail wands, rattling their rattles, singing and chanting. As Big Arrow began to pale and sway in the saddle, someone beckoned to Ta-boodle. (He had been watching from a distance but according to tribal custom did not offer assistance until invited by the Buffalo Medicine Men.)

Once Ta-boodle took charge, he washed the wound with water from a nearby pond and gave Big Arrow a drink. However, the water came out the hole in the wounded man's throat. Ta-boodle then held one hand over the wound and gave Big Arrow more water. Big Arrow downed the water and immediately threw up the blood he had swallowed. This pleased Ta-boodle and he gave Big Arrow more water to "flush him out again." Ta-boodle then cleaned the wound with a piece of soft wood and fashioned a small cup from the soft fibers of a dead cottonwood tree. He drew the edges of the wound together under the cup, covered it with tallow, and tied it in place. After Big Arrow rested for about an hour, Ta-boodle gave him a little broth made from buffalo jerky. With his knife, he then removed the bullet lodged in the shoulder. Ta-boodle also dressed this wound with buffalo tallow and a wooden cup. In time, Big Arrow recovered, although he had

Ta-boodle's gravestone stands in the Kiowa-Comanche-Apache Cemetery at the Kiowa Baptist Church near Saddle Mountain, Oklahoma. His name cannot be rendered precisely in English and as a result appears in many forms in historical writings and yet a different form on his grave.

terrible scars. He lived to be about ninety and wore a black eye patch the rest of his life.

Ta-boodle tended to other injuries besides war wounds. In 1865, a boy named Tap-to suffered a broken leg. It was a complicated compound fracture. Tap-to's parents took him to Ta-boodle after the medicine men's treatment failed. Ta-boodle studied the injury then made a cradle splint from dogwood branches. He manipulated the leg until he had the bones fairly well aligned, then placed the leg in the dogwood splint and tied it securely. After wearing the splint for quite some time the boy recovered completely without a limp.

Ta-boodle also treated rattlesnake bites. Instead of applying the herbal cures that Indians were known to use, he enlarged the fang marks with his knife and sucked the poison from the wound with his mouth. When all the poison had been removed and spat on the ground, Ta-boodle sprinkled gunpowder on the cuts and ignited the powder with a match. This seared (cauterized) the wound to stop the bleeding and offered some protection against infection.

Ta-boodle's long life ended September 15, 1901. Although he was not a member of the church, he is buried at the Saddle Mountain Kiowa Baptist Church cemetery, now known as the Saddle Mountain Intertribal Burial Ground. According to Dr. Parker, "Cemeteries located at various Indian churches or former church sites are property of the Kiowa, Comanche and Kiowa-Apache tribes." For this reason many Indians are buried in church cemeteries although they were not church members.

Ta-boodle was a member of many war parties, where he often proved to be the best and last hope of a wounded comrade. In his long life he earned the respect of his people as a gifted healer. By using heroic methods to save lives, he introduced the Kiowa to the possibility of combining traditional medicine with newer methods of healing.

COYOTE WOMAN, STAYS YELLOW, AND MRS. GOOD BEAR

Mandan Medicine Women
(d. 1945)

The Mandan Indians lived on the northern Plains in the territory presently occupied by the state of North Dakota. It was the Dakota Indians who referred to them as Mandan. They, however, called themselves Numakiki, meaning "people." Early in the eighteenth century, about 3,500 Mandan Indians occupied nine villages on the Missouri River near the mouth of the Heart River.

The Mandan built their villages on high bluffs, protected by the river on one side and stockades and barrier ditches on the other. They lived in lodges made from willow branches and grass interwoven over a wooden frame and plastered with mud and clay. In some villages, as many as 150 of these earthen lodges circled an open area used for dances, ceremonies, and other tribal gatherings. With a diameter of 40 feet, each lodge housed two or three families.

Within the Mandan community, members of each family owned individual medicine bundles and tended to the family's medical needs. Traditionally, all Mandan women were healers. Like many mothers of today, their duties included nursing and first aid. Until the arrival of the white explorers who introduced foreign diseases, the Indians had remedies for most ailments common to them. In fact, many of the medicines we use today, such as aspirin, were actually present in the herbs, roots, and barks the Indians used. When sickness was too severe for family cures, the tribal doctor (medicine man or woman thought to have supernatural powers) was called on to perform healing rites. These doctors received their supernatural powers in a vision or dream.

Through the writings of Alfred Bowers, an ethnologist for the Smithsonian Institution who studied the Mandan culture in 1930–31, we know of three generations of Mandan medicine women within one family: Coyote Woman, Stays Yellow, and Mrs. Good Bear.

Coyote Woman, considered to be a powerful Mandan medicine woman, received the right to treat the illnesses of her people from a dream. She did not pass these doctoring rights on to her daughter, Stays Yellow. Stays Yellow received her own doctoring rights, limited to treating women in difficult labor, from her own dream. She passed these rights on to her daughter, Mrs. Good Bear.

No birth records of any of these women exist. Indians did not count years. Instead, they remembered their age by a significant event. Mrs. Good Bear's memory offers the only clue to the date of her birth. She remembered that she was grown and married when Custer and his men passed near the Mandan village on their way to Little Bighorn. Custer and his men rode into an Indian ambush and were killed at this famous battle, fought in 1876, known as Custer's Last Stand. From this information, Alfred

Bowers determined that Mrs. Good Bear was born between 1850 and 1860. Accordingly, her mother and grandmother, Stays Yellow and Coyote Woman, would have been born sometime in the first half of the nineteenth century, a generation apart.

Basically an agricultural tribe, the Mandan hunted and traded surplus corn to the Assiniboine, another Plains tribe, for additional buffalo hides and meat. In the communal Mandan tribe, the young learned specific skills from the old. Whether farming, hunting, or lodge building, each person made an essential contribution to the tribe and culture. The 1837 smallpox epidemic struck the tribe with great force, killing all but 150 of the 1,800 Mandan. The massive death toll resulted in the loss of so much tribal knowledge that the few who survived could not provide for themselves. In an attempt to sustain life, the Mandan survivors joined members of the neighboring Hidatsa tribe. Although they strove to maintain tribal identity, much of the culture of each tribe was lost forever. In 1845 they moved north to form a new village at a bend in the Missouri River, which they called Like-a-Fishhook.

Bowers recorded Mrs. Good Bear's account of the lives of her mother and grandmother in his book *Mandan Social and Ceremonial Organization.*

Mrs. Good Bear's grandmother, Coyote Woman, was a medicine woman. She received doctoring rights when a large bear came to her in a dream. According to Mrs. Good Bear, the bear said to Coyote Woman, "You must go among your people doctoring. People will give you white buffalo robes, leggings, dresses, and moccasins, for you will cure all who ask your help." The Mandan believed Coyote Woman possessed strong medicine because she saw a bear in her dream. Mrs. Good Bear said, "We have always believed . . . that the bear was the greatest of all doctors."

After this dream, Coyote Woman began treating the sick people of her tribe. She examined her patients and believed that some were made ill by snakes or bugs in their bodies. She determined that some were under the influence of evil spirits and others had lost their god. In her attempts to cure her patients, she sang a medicine song and used a medicine root in various ways. Roots with medicinal properties were sometimes made into a beverage or were chewed and placed on the sick person. Mrs. Good Bear said, "If she [Coyote Woman] found the pain was in one spot, she sucked with her mouth or a hollow horn, sometimes drawing out long slim worms or maggots of different colors. She pressed the stomach for pains located in the stomach or bowels and blew chewed-up cedar bark over the patient." If a person came to Coyote Woman with a headache, she "let out blood from the head."

Coyote Woman probably knew more about sleight of hand and illusion than physical healing. However, at least some of her patients recovered and the Mandan had faith in Coyote Woman's healing power. She achieved her success, in part, because Indians had a generally healthy lifestyle, which included natural food, fresh air, unpolluted water, and plenty of exercise. Her patients had strong healthy bodies that recovered from injuries and illnesses common to them. In addition, their faith in the supernatural power of the medicine ritual promoted healing. Modern researchers have proved that negative attitudes can cause serious illness, while positive attitudes, faith, and prayer can bring about healing.

The Mandan, like other Indian tribes, had a strong faith in their medicine men and women. Today, those who practice modern medicine on reservations find that their patients recover better when medical care includes traditional tribal religious beliefs as well as scientific treatment.

Stays Yellow listened many times as Coyote Woman told of her cures; however, Coyote Woman did not pass her doctoring rights on to Stays Yellow. Like other young Mandan women, Stays Yellow fasted, seeking a vision for herself.

According to Mandan tradition, both men and women fasted. The Mandan believed that those who suffered during fasting received stronger power. Men sometimes increased their suffering by cutting themselves, but women seldom did this. Women were not believed to need strong powers and they did not fast in the same places as men. Men fasted in the ceremonial lodge, while women usually fasted in their gardens, on the corn scaffolds, or in the woods.

When Stays Yellow decided to fast, she went into the woods. Alone through the night and possibly frightened, she fell asleep just before daylight and had a dream. She saw an old man and woman, a young woman struggling to give birth, and several dead watersnakes. The old man shook a leather rattle decorated with white feathers as he and the old woman sang a medicine song. The old woman chewed black root (also called black medicine) they had dug in the forest. She blew the chewed root over the snakes. As the black root touched them, they came to life and slithered away. The last one, swollen with young, responded slowly. The old woman blew the black root on her again and again. Each time the chewed root touched the pregnant snake, a young snake was born. After the last snake slithered away, the old couple told Stays Yellow she could doctor women when they had difficult labor.

After receiving this vision, Stays Yellow collected all the items seen in her vision and wrapped them in a small piece of animal skin. This would be her medicine bundle. It contained dried black root and sage. Stays Yellow did not include the leather rattle in her medicine bundle because it belonged to a man. She also committed to memory the medicine song sung by the woman in her vision and remembered it for the rest of her life.

Black root comes from a plant that grows in moist, wooded areas. A member of the figwort family, the plant is indigenous to North America. The Mandan found many uses for black root. They used the chewed root to cover open wounds and sometimes spread it on the body of a sick person. Other times they boiled the root to make a tea. Today it is known to work as an antiseptic when applied to a wound and a strong laxative when drunk as a tea. Black medicine had fewer side effects than the calomel white doctors used for purging their patients. Given during labor, the tea would have assisted in the birth process by contracting the bowel and stomach muscles. After delivery it would have purged the system and helped the mother's bodily functions return to normal. Chewed root, blown over the patient, may have served as an antiseptic. Or, the rite may have served as a visible treatment that stimulated the patient's religious faith. Red sage represented the sun and white sage represented the moon. The Mandan burned sage to purify the lodge in preparation for childbirth. They used sage in most doctoring rites.

Since she had seen watersnakes in her dream, Stays Yellow considered them to be special. According to Mrs. Good Bear, Stays Yellow "never killed snakes after that; she always blew some of the medicine root on any snake near our lodge and then carried it away."

Stays Yellow did not have the opportunity to use her medicine bundle until she was quite old. According to her daughter, Mrs. Good Bear, "She [Stays Yellow] learned of a woman [struggling to give birth] that other doctors had given up to die and went to help her. The woman was scarcely alive but still conscious and could talk a little."

Stays Yellow told the woman undergoing labor that she had no great supernatural powers but she would do just as she had seen in her dream. She chewed the black root and blew it over the laboring woman. She sang the medicine song she heard in her dream. When the woman failed to deliver the child, Stays Yellow asked for a stiff feather. She then raised the laboring woman's head and placed her knee against the woman's abdomen. She opened the woman's mouth and forced the feather down her throat. As the woman gagged, her stomach muscles tightened and Stays Yellow assisted the contraction with pressure from her knee. The child was born the fourth time Stays Yellow forced the feather down the mother's throat. (Raising the head and shoulders and applying pressure is one method of assisting in chidlbirth still in use today.) After the delivery, Stays Yellow gave the mother a tea brewed from the black root to drink.

She received a horse, ten blankets, and many yards of calico for helping the mother deliver a healthy child.

When Stays Yellow helped the woman through her difficult labor, she performed the ritual she had learned in her dream. However, when the child was not delivered, she used her knowledge gained from personal experience to assist the mother. Through her own childbirth experience and acting as midwife in her family, Stays Yellow probably had learned enough to understand that tightening the stomach muscles and adding pressure on the uterus would help deliver the child. Mrs. Good Bear explained, "My mother did not dream that she should use the feather. It was her own idea . . ."

Most Mandan women gave birth easily, with only the help of the women in the family. Women knew about the physical aspects of labor and delivery and were skilled enough to turn an unborn child or manipulate it into a better position for delivery. A tribal doctor (owner of a medicine bundle) was only called to attend in difficult deliveries. With doctors receiving such high payment, few Mandan could afford these services except as a last resort. The most sought after doctors owned bundles given by the snake, bear, or mink. Stays Yellow's medicine came from the snake.

Stays Yellow did not attend women who were having difficulty in childbirth until after she reached menopause because the Mandan believed that if a menstruating woman entered the lodge, the sick person might die. In fact, all menstruating women were asked to stay away from the lodge. If one accidentally entered the premises, sage was immediately burned in four places to cleanse the lodge. Two fires burned red sage and two fires burned white sage. A special song accompanied the burning of the sage and the doctor received payment for singing this song. While the sage burned and the doctor sang the special song, two young girls were called to attend the patient instead. They sang and danced around the laboring woman.

To request the services of a doctor to perform sacred rites, the women of the family filled a pipe. They placed the pipe before the doctor (almost always a woman) they wished to attend the birth. At this time, the family agreed to carry out the doctor's instructions and to pay a set price for a certain number of days that the doctor would attend the patient. If the doctor failed to deliver the baby in the agreed time, she would leave and give another doctor a chance to treat the patient. Sometimes, however, the family set the pipe before the doctor a second time, asking her to continue her treatment. If she stayed longer, an additional fee was paid.

Women usually gave birth on a robe laid on the floor near the bed posts. The laboring woman could grip the bed posts and pull

Mrs. Good Bear with one of her children.   (Library of Congress)

during hard contractions. After delivery, the doctor bound the mother's abdomen with a wide belt.

The doctor attending the mother chose an old woman in the tribe to care for the newborn. To prevent chafing, Mandan babies were rubbed with red ocher (iron ore) under the arms, around the neck, between the legs, and on top of the head. They were greased, probably with buffalo fat, to protect the skin from irritation and insect bites. The Mandan powdered the diaper area with pounded buffalo chips. The baby was then wrapped in soft hide taken from the smoke hole, because this leather would not stiffen when it became wet. Placed in a leather cradleboard shortly after birth, the infant remained in the cradleboard during the day but slept with its mother at night. The mother removed the baby from the cradleboard twice a day. At this time, she nursed, cleaned, and greased the baby.

Strapped to mother's back or propped against a tree, the child could nap or watch family activities from the cradleboard. Although styles varied from tribe to tribe, almost all Indians used the cradleboard. These efficient infant carriers made from tree branches and leather not only kept Indian babies in the center of family life, but also made them ready for quick travel. More than one story has surfaced of a young father gripping a cradleboard strap in his teeth and a rifle in his hands as he ran for safety during a surprise enemy attack.

Pioneer infants were wrapped in cloth instead of tanned hides and slept in rocking cradles instead of cradleboards. Pioneer and Indian women, however, faced the same challenges giving birth on the Plains. Indian women with midwifery skills sometimes attended pioneer women during childbirth. Few doctors were available on the frontier. American women of the nineteenth and early twentieth centuries who lived in settled areas, however, feared hospitals and the dread childbed fever. In fact, women who gave birth in hospitals were more likely to die from infection than from complications of birth. At that time, medical doctors did not understand germs and infection. They went from patient to patient, and sometimes from the morgue to the delivery room, without washing their hands. The germs on their hands caused childbed fever and many new mothers died from this terrible infection.

Indian women who acted as midwives also knew nothing about germs. However, attending few births, one at a time, they did not carry germs from one patient to another. The new mothers they attended did not get childbed fever.

No record of Stays Yellow's death has been found. We only know that she passed her doctoring rights on to her daughter. Mrs. Good Bear said, "My mother turned her doctoring bundle over to me when she was old."

Mrs. Good Bear reported using the medicine bundle only once. She entered the lodge and, according to Mandan custom, immediately asked everyone to leave except the laboring woman and her mother. Next, Mrs. Good Bear closed the door and pulled the flap partially across the smoke hole to darken the room. As the sick woman's labor continued, Mrs. Good Bear began to follow her mother's instructions. She sang the medicine song and chewed the dried black root from her medicine bundle. She then blew the chewed black root over the expectant mother. Mrs. Good Bear took more black root from her medicine bundle and brewed a medicinal tea. The laboring woman drank the brew and the child was born before Mrs. Good Bear had time to carry out the rest of her mother's doctoring instructions. In payment for her services, Mrs. Good Bear received a fat steer.

No records exist of the births or deaths of Coyote Woman and Stays Yellow, although it is known that Mrs. Good Bear lived to be about ninety years old. After her marriage to Good Bear, a Hidatsa, she participated in important tribal ceremonies and became a prominent member of the Hidatsa tribe. A devout Catholic in her later years, she probably abandoned her Mandan name and became Mrs. Good Bear when she was baptized. She died in North Dakota, October 10, 1945.

The lives of Coyote Woman, Stays Yellow, and Mrs. Good Bear span the nineteenth century and extend into the twentieth century. A record of these women's lives survives only because Mrs. Good Bear related her story to Alfred Bowers. From her memories, we know something about childbirth and infant care among the Mandans.

SWIMMER

Cherokee Medicine Man
(c. 1835–99)

As the nineteenth century opened, the Cherokee were the largest and most powerful tribe in the Southeast. Occupying a large area covering the western Carolinas, northern Georgia, and Tennessee, they readily accepted white influence. Like white southerners, they plowed fields, grew crops, raised farm animals, readied their cotton and wool for market, and owned slaves. They frequently adopted whites into the tribe and intermarriage became common. They founded schools and brought in white teachers. They established their own constitutional government in 1827. Still, the Cherokee, North America's most assimilated tribe, would be a casualty of white civilization as it spread west, gobbling up Indian land by means of various treaties.

With their acceptance of white ways, many Cherokee lost faith in the medicine man and began to visit white doctors. Old traditions and customs faded from the memory of all but an unwavering few. One such Cherokee, Swimmer, was a healer who preserved the ancient arts of spiritual and herbal medicine.

In 1835, Eastern Cherokee lands fell victim to a final and devastating blow. Against the will of the majority, leaders of a small group within the tribe signed the Treaty of New Echota. This treaty transferred 7 million acres of Cherokee land to the United States government for an initial sum of $5 million plus resettlement compensations to be paid later. The treaty required that the Cherokee move westward within three years.

As the 1838 deadline for removal neared, federal soldiers forcefully removed Cherokee families from their homes. Most Cherokees resigned themselves to this fate; however, many of those who still held to the old tradition managed to escape into the Great Smoky Mountains. In one incident, an old man named Charlie watched helplessly as soldiers prodded his ailing wife along at the sharp point of a bayonet. In despair, Charlie, his brother, and three sons overpowered their captors and the family escaped to the mountains. Unfortunately, a soldier was killed in their struggle for freedom.

Determined to punish the culprits, General Scott (the federal officer in charge of the Cherokee roundup) offered freedom to the other escapees in exchange for the surrender of Charlie and his men. Immediately shot upon surrender, their sacrifice gained freedom for the small band that later became known as the Eastern Cherokee. The elders of the Eastern band held to tradition and worked to preserve the ancient Cherokee knowledge.

Swimmer (Ayunini), about three years old at the time, was among those Eastern Cherokee who settled in North Carolina. One of the youngest of those who escaped to the mountains, Swimmer grew up under the instruction of tribal masters. After years of training he became a priest, doctor, and keeper of tradition.

Swimmer was born about 1835, somewhere in the vast Cherokee lands in the Southeast that were lost in the Treaty of Echota (signed in the year of his birth). The fate of his parents is unknown. Educated among his people, Swimmer learned to write and read Cherokee using the alphabet invented by Sequoya in 1827. In fact, the Cherokee alphabet fit the language so well that almost all Cherokee could read and write a few months after the creation of the alphabet. Destined to be a medicine man from an early age,

Swimmer began learning from the masters during his childhood. In all probability, according to Cherokee tradition, an old priest "examined the beads" to determine Swimmer's destiny. When examining the beads, the medicine man rolled two beads of different colors between his thumb and finger. The color of the bead that worked its way further down his finger determined the answer to a yes or no question.

As a student, Swimmer probably listened to the mythkeepers and priests as they recited traditions and discussed their secret knowledge late into the night. He may have tended the fire in the sleeping house where these elders gathered. After a long night of listening, Swimmer and other students would have accompanied priests to a nearby running stream at daybreak. In a ceremony called "going to the water," the priests scratched the naked skin of the students with a bone-tooth comb. Then the students waded out into the stream, faced the rising sun, and submerged themselves seven times while the priests recited prayers on shore. This purification rite, which includes "scratching" and "going to the water," is also a part of the ball play and green-corn dance ceremonies.

The Cherokee performed the Green-Corn Dance, a thanksgiving ceremony, before eating the first ears of a new corn crop. Competitive ball play took the place of battle after the Cherokee laid down their arms in the late 1770s. The team, led by a medicine man, prepared for the competition. At daybreak, the medicine man scratched each player with a seven-toothed scratching comb made from the sharpened splinters of a turkey leg bone. Twenty-eight 6-inch scratches were made on the upper arms, forearms, thighs, lower legs, breast, and back. In all, each ball player received nearly 300 shallow gashes. While the blood flowed, the medicine man rubbed herbal medicine into the open wounds to strengthen the players' muscles. The ball players then "went to the water" along with the ball sticks to be used in the play. While the ball players immersed themselves in the running stream four to seven times, the medicine man stayed on the bank and examined the beads. Ball play was as much a competition between medicine men as between teams.

Swimmer (Ayuini), wearing his turban and carrying his rattle in a photo taken by James Mooney on the Qualla Reservation, North Carolina, 1888. (Smithsonian Institution Photo No. 1008)

Ball play had been a part of the preparation for battle since ancient times. It would again serve its ancient purpose during the Civil War when the Cherokee enlisted in the Confederate army. In 1862, William H. Thomas, a longtime trusted friend, recruited the Eastern Cherokee to serve in the Confederate army. About 400 Cherokee, almost every able-bodied man, enlisted to serve under white officers in the Thomas Legion. Swimmer served in Cherokee Company A of the Sixty-ninth Regiment.

The war provided an opportunity to practice old cultural ceremonies. Wearing the Confederate uniform, the Cherokee soldiers held war dances sporting feathers and paint. They also held the ceremonial ball play before going on patrol. In his late twenties at the time, Second Sergeant Swimmer probably served as tribal priest and medicine man during the ceremonies as well as doctor to the Cherokee soldiers.

Assigned to scouting and home-guard details in the mountain region along the Tennessee-Carolina border, the Cherokee soldiers saw little combat. At the end of the war, however, they received recognition for "good work and service for the South."

In a lengthy legal struggle after the war, the Eastern Cherokee gained title to 65,000 acres in North Carolina and formed a tribal corporation in 1889. Many of them still live on or near the Qualla Reservation in North Carolina.

In 1887, James Mooney, ethnologist for the Smithsonian Institution, decided to study the Cherokee. He found the culture all but lost among the Western Cherokee in Oklahoma. However, the culture still existed on the Qualla Reservation in North Carolina. Swimmer served as a consultant to James Mooney in 1887 and 1888. Through his disclosure of sacred formulas and prescriptions, Swimmer revealed the ancient knowledge of Cherokee medicine.

Swimmer based his medical practice on an ancient myth that the Cherokee believed explained the causes of diseases and their cures. According to this myth, long ago, when animals could talk, people and animals lived together in peace. As the human race increased, their settlements spread over the whole earth, crowding the animals. The humans invented weapons and began to kill the larger animals for meat and skins. Smaller creatures were crushed underfoot in carelessness and contempt. Species by species, the animals met in council to devise a plan of revenge against the humans and limit their number. The bears decided to fight with their natural weapons, teeth and claws. The deer, however, decided to inflict rheumatism upon any hunter who killed one of them. The fishes and reptiles also held a meeting and decided to make their victims dream of eating decaying fish or snakes winding about them to blow bad breath in their faces. As a result, the victims would lose their appetite, sicken, and die. Finally, the birds, insects, and smaller animals met. One by one, they each named a disease to be inflicted upon the humans—so many that, without some defense against the diseases, the human race would have been wiped out.

Fortunately, the plants were friendly to humans. When they heard the animals' plan, they decided to come to the humans' rescue. Every living plant, from the tallest tree to the smallest moss, agreed to provide a remedy for one of the diseases the animals inflicted. According to Mooney's record of Swimmer's account of this myth, "the plants, every one of which has its use if we only knew it, furnish the antidote to counteract the evil wrought by the revengeful animals. When the doctor is in doubt what treatment to apply for the relief of a patient, the spirit of the plant suggests to him the proper remedy."

No one really has any better explanation for how the Indians knew which plants to use to remedy certain ailments. Some were found by trial and error, others because the appearance of the plant seemed related to the disease. For example, when the patient vomited yellow bile (white doctors used the term "biliousness" and the Cherokee word for the same symptom meant yellow), the Cherokee doctor made his medicine from yellow roots, stems, or flowers of four different herbs and administered the concoction with a ceremonial rite and song (prayer).

In the twentieth century, scientists discovered that although faith played a major role in healing, many plants used by Indian doctors indeed contained curative substances. Indian doctors often blew medicine on their patients or rubbed it on the afflicted area, whereas white doctors prescribed the same medicines to be swallowed. Those who practiced modern medicine at the time scoffed at the Indian's practice of applying medicines to the skin. A century later, however, the medicated patch, which allows a substance to be absorbed slowly through the skin, is recognized as an efficient means of administering medicine.

In many cases, the song and attention of the medicine man may have offered more healing power than the herbal concoction. Mooney wrote in the late 1800s that "the Indian has . . . implicit confidence in the shaman [medicine man]. The ceremonies and prayers are well calculated to inspire this feeling, and the effect thus produced upon the mind of the sick man undoubtedly reacts favorably upon his physical organization."

Traditionally, Cherokee medicine men memorized the formulas and transferred them verbally to trusted peers. Sometimes the formulas were purchased and other times traded. The exchange of formulas took place in secret. One medicine man would say to the other, "Let us sit down together," which meant, "Let us tell each other our secrets." If the second medicine man agreed they would go to a secluded spot and exchange information. Mooney wrote that the medicine men guarded their formulas carefully and when "performing the ceremonies the words used are uttered in such a low tone of voice as to be unintelligible even to the one for whose benefit the formula is repeated."

While studying the Cherokee culture, Mooney was impressed with Swimmer's knowledge and intelligence. He spent several days listening to Swimmer's accounts of Cherokee myths. When Swimmer completed one story that included a reference to sacred songs, Mooney asked him if he knew the songs. Swimmer said he did, but would not repeat the songs because they were a part of his secret knowledge. He commented further that hunters paid him a high price, as much as $5 for a single song, "because you can't kill any bears or deer unless you sing them." Mooney explained that he wanted to record and preserve the songs so that the world would know how much the Cherokee had known. This interested Swimmer. Mooney then added that medicine men of other tribes had sent their songs to Washington. Swimmer promptly declared that he knew as much as any of them and agreed to give Mooney all his information so that others could judge who, among the medicine men, knew the most.

When the other Cherokee medicine men heard of this, they took desperate measures in an attempt to stop Swimmer from revealing the sacred formulas. They spread rumors to undermine Swimmer's character and integrity. When this failed, they tried to convince Swimmer that when the information was taken to Washington his knowledge would leave him. This worried Swimmer, and Mooney was unable to devise a way to disprove the claim. Within a few days, however, Swimmer presented a small book to Mooney. "Look at that and now see if I don't know something," he said proudly.

It was a small notebook of about 240 pages, about half filled with Cherokee writing. A brief examination revealed it contained the information Mooney had been wanting. He wrote, "Here were prayers, songs, and prescriptions for the cure of all kinds of diseases—for chills, rheumatism, frostbites, wounds, bad dreams . . . prayers for long life, for safety among strangers, for acquiring influence in council and success in ball play . . . It was in fact an Indian ritual and pharmacopoeia."

Prior to seeing Swimmer's book, Mooney thought all knowledge of Cherokee medicine existed only in the memories of medicine men. However, when the Cherokee alphabet came into use, medicine men began to write their formulas in small books they carried in secret.

Mooney immediately persuaded Swimmer to copy his formulas in a blank book he provided. He then arranged to purchase the original that he deposited in the library of the Bureau of Ethnology.

Most of Swimmer's formulas contained a song, or prayer, to be sung over the patient, and instructions for preparing medicines from plants. He explained the details of each formula to Mooney.

Sometimes, along with the treatment, the patient had to avoid certain foods or contact with certain things. For example, if, according to myth, squirrels caused the illness, the patient refrained from eating squirrel meat. Those who suffered rheumatism were instructed to avoid eating the leg of any animal because the disease usually affected the limbs. The seriously ill patient was isolated to avoid any possible contact with a pregnant or menstruating woman or anyone who might have come from a house where such a woman lived. Such contact was thought to make the doctor's treatment ineffective.

Based on the myth explaining the cause of disease, Swimmer and other medicine men sought out the cause of the disease by questioning the patient about his dreams and any taboos he may have violated. These taboos included urinating in the river, spitting on a fire, and failing to ask a bear's pardon for killing it. Once the cause was determined, the medicine man set out to gather the herbs and roots for the cure. Upon acquiring his supply, Swimmer prepared the medicine and administered the treatment, which usually lasted four to seven days.

In general, the doctor did not charge for his services, and any payment he received was considered a gift. Long ago, this gift was a deer skin or a pair of moccasins. In Swimmer's time, it was a certain amount of cloth, a garment, or handkerchief. In addition, some of the formulas required the use of a certain amount of cloth. After the treatment, the medicine man sold or gave this cloth away to prevent the death of the patient.

As the Cherokees accepted white civilization, they began to lose confidence in the medicine men and sought treatment from white doctors. The medicine men resisted this loss of authority and devised a way to keep their patients. Declaring the white doctor's medicine poison to Indians, they prescribed a four-year course of Indian treatment to eliminate the poison from the system.

Although Swimmer had little knowledge of the true cause of disease and treatment, many of the herbs and roots he used were also used by white doctors. However, the uses and methods frequently differed. Swimmer and other medicine men often chewed and blew the medicines on the skin of their patients while white doctors more often prepared concoctions to be taken internally. White doctors learned the uses of herbs by trial and error, while the Indians chose their medicinal plants by simple logic. For example, a plant commonly called queen of the meadow, or gravel

gravel root, is considered by herbalists as a good remedy for ridding the kidneys or bladder of small gravel or mineral accumulations. The Cherokee boiled the roots of this plant to obtain a decoction given to relieve difficult urination. They made this logical choice because "water can be sucked up through its hollow stalk." Over time the medicine proved successful and became a part of Cherokee pharmacology.

Some medicine men specialized in a certain area of treatment. However, Swimmer's notebook recorded not only cures but also formulas for successful hunts, romance, and dealing with enemies. Written in the Cherokee language, the notebook offered the first example of Indian thought. Mooney wrote that the notebook was "invaluable as the genuine production of the Indian mind, setting forth in the clearest light the state of the aboriginal religion before its contamination by contact with whites." For the first time, the Indian was seen as essentially pious and thoughtful, mindful of his religion in every act of his daily life.

Cherokee formulas contain prayer and prescription. The Cherokee did not worship a Great Spirit or believe in life after death. They prayed to the spirits of animals, birds, fish, and plants, and used natural enemies in battle against the causes of their illnesses.

Among his people, Swimmer was held in high esteem. In going about his duties, he constantly traveled about the community, treating the sick, gathering plants for medicine, and answering the call to help solve personal problems and assure successful endeavors. He participated in tribal functions, including green-corn dances and ball play. Trained in ancient tradition and included in every aspect of tribal life, he became one of the most knowledgeable and influential people in the tribe.

Swimmer died in March 1899 at the age of sixty-five. He was buried on the slope of a forest-clad mountain according to Cherokee tradition. James Mooney wrote in memorial to Swimmer, "Peace to his ashes and sorrow for his going, for with him perished half the tradition of a people."

Mooney considered Swimmer a genuine aboriginal antiquarian, or a good example of the Cherokee people of the past and a conservator of their traditions. A true patriot, Swimmer was proud of his people and their ancient culture. Swimmer did not speak English and "to the day of his death clung to the moccasin and turban, together with the rattle, his badge of authority. Through him, a window opened to the past preserving knowledge of the Cherokee culture thought lost to this civilized tribe."

CARLOS MONTEZUMA

Yavapai Apache Physician
(c. 1866–1923)

Before resigning from his job with the Indian Health Service, Dr. Carlos Montezuma wrote to a good friend in Chicago to ask his opinion of his plan to go into private practice. The friend replied, "Well, doctor, I would advise you to stick to the government job where the pay is sure. If you come to Chicago I am afraid you will not make a success here because there will be prejudice against you, even though you may be the best physician—you are an Indian."

Later, Montezuma described his feelings when he read those words: "My Apache blood rushed into my head, and I said, 'God helping me, I will resign the government service and go back to Chicago and fight prejudice.'"

With this mindset, he resigned from the Indian Health Service and applied for an Illinois medical license in 1896. He joined a practice located in the prestigious Chicago Loop area and put into effect the ideal he would later promote in his speeches: "Make good, deliver the goods, and convince the world by your character that the Indians are not as they have been misrepresented to be." Thus, Dr. Montezuma began his fight against prejudice and for Indian rights.

Born in the Superstition Mountains of Arizona about 1866, Wassaja, a Yavapai child, would be known throughout most of his life as Carlos Montezuma, a full-blood Apache. (The Yavapai were also known as Mohave Apache, although they were not true Apache.)

Carlos later remembered his father, Cocuyevah, as a prominent warrior, "five feet, six or seven inches in height, very broad and muscular, with a wide forehead, and hair cut to the shoulders and parted in the middle, according to the customs of many Indian tribes." He also wrote of his mother, later identified by biographer Peter Iverson as Thilgeyah: "My mother's name I have forgotten. She was taller than father. I remember her as being a good mother, and I often thought when I saw Indian children orphans that if my mother were dead I would rather die than live."

Young Wassaja lived with his people until 1871. At that time, the Pima, an enemy tribe that lived nearby, attacked the Yavapai camp at Iron Top Mountain. During the attack, the Pima took Wassaja and several other youngsters captive. That night, the Pima stood their captives before a fire that blazed high above the treetops. Carlos later remembered his terror: "There were thirteen of us standing in a row . . . I thought that this big fire was for us. I imagined I could hear my flesh sizzle."

As it turned out, the Pima had not intended to harm their captives. An Apache could be sold for much money and this may explain how Carlos Montezuma's Yavapai identity became temporarily obscured. The Pima sold the young "Apache" to Carlos Gentile, a traveling Italian-American photographer, for $30.

The next morning, Gentile took Wassaja to the water well to be washed. Years later, Montezuma wrote about his first bath: "This was done in a tub, and this was my first step toward civilization." In the care of Carlos Gentile, Wassaja began a new life—leaving his people, his land, and his name.

Gentile had Wassaja baptized Carlos Montezuma at the Church of the Assumption, in Florence, Arizona Territory, on November 17, 1871. Gentile renamed the boy Carlos, after himself, and Montezuma, in recognition of Wassaja's Indian heritage and the land of his birth. (Many ancient Indian sites in central Arizona are named in honor of Montezuma, a famous Aztec ruler.)

His baptismal certificate lists Carlos Montezuma's date of birth as 1866, although he may have been born in 1865. Montezuma usually gave his birthdate as 1867.

Gentile took Carlos east. They made their way on horseback and by stagecoach across Indian Territory to the railroad near Pueblo, Colorado. There they boarded the train and traveled on, visiting Denver, Chicago, Washington, New York, Detroit, and Grand Rapids. After about six months they settled in Chicago, where Carlos attended public schools.

Carlos remained with Gentile for several years. But when fire destroyed Gentile's business, he faced financial ruin and decided he could no longer care for the boy. For a while, Carlos moved from one home to another. Then in 1878, when Carlos was about eleven years old, George Ingalls, a Baptist missionary, became his caretaker.

Ingalls had a plan for Carlos Montezuma's future. He wanted him to become " . . . a real Christian and then to be a physician and with a good education and love of Christ in his heart, to go back to his people and labor for their good . . ." In order to carry out this plan, Ingalls placed Carlos in the care of William H. Stedman, a Baptist minister.

A good student who learned quickly, Montezuma began preparing for college. At that time, few people went to college, and Carlos Montezuma would be among the first Indians to attend. He entered the Preparatory School (a private high school) in 1879 and later attended the University of Illinois. While at college, Montezuma became secretary of the Adelphics, one of three University of Illinois debate teams. He gained recognition for his speeches, particularly for one about Indian bravery.

Montezuma worked on a farm to pay his way through college. After earning a bachelor of science degree in chemistry, he enrolled at Chicago Medical College at Northwestern University in 1885. He worked part time in a drug store near the school where his duties included washing windows and general cleaning. He struggled through medical school with little money to spare, devoting most of his time and energy to his studies.

Discouraged by the difficulties he faced, Montezuma sought advice from Richard Henry Pratt, founder of Carlisle Indian School (the first off-reservation school for Indian children) in Pennsylvania. Pratt replied that "this world is full of work for those who will undertake it." He encouraged Montezuma to continue working toward his medical degree. Pratt believed that Indians had to leave the old way behind and become a part of modern industrial America. In his view, an educated Carlos Montezuma could make a difference in the lives of his people. As an Indian achieving success in the white people's world, he could set an example for others to follow.

Although Montezuma completed his studies in 1888, the faculty withheld his diploma until 1889 for no apparent cause. Through this year of disappointment, Pratt encouraged Montezuma to "press forward where the Indians ought to be—man among men." In years to come, as Montezuma fought for Indian rights, being a man among men would be one of his credos.

After receiving his M.D., Montezuma decided to establish a private practice. He opened an office near Chicago Medical College; however, few patients were willing to come to the new doctor. As Montezuma struggled with his new practice, Pratt put in a good word for him with Commissioner of Indian Affairs Thomas Jefferson Morgan. As a result, Morgan offered Dr. Montezuma a position within the Indian Service. Montezuma accepted the position adding that, "Nothing else would give me greater pleasure."

Although he had been away from his homeland most of his life and had not seen a reservation, Montezuma sensed that the Indians now faced both opportunity and danger. While assimilation offered education, Christianity, and the chance to pursue a chosen career, it also posed a threat. As white settlers crossed the frontier, some sought to cheat unsuspecting Indians out of their lands and natural resources.

Morgan appointed Montezuma to the position of clerk and physician at the Indian school at Fort Stevenson, Dakota Territory

Carlos Montezuma fought against prejudice and for Indian rights.
(Smithsonian Institution Photo No. 53,534)

in 1889. He received an annual salary of $1,000 (fair pay for the late 1800s). While working as a doctor in the Indian Service, Montezuma served at two other reservations, the Western Shoshone Reservation in Nevada and the Colville Agency in Washington.

Dr. Montezuma found his people living in unacceptable conditions. Removed from their hunting grounds and restricted to reservations, nothing remained of their old way of life. And yet the Indians received none of the benefits of white civilization.

With the passage of the General Allotment Act in 1887, each Indian received 80 acres. The allotted land, however, proved to be near worthless to the Indians. Without tools or the knowledge to use them, they could not live off the land. To make life even more difficult, they had no money and no houses. Denied the old way and unable to take advantage of the new way, the Indians could no longer provide for themselves. The government issued monthly allotments of food and clothing and provided limited medical care, but the Indians had no hospitals and insufficient medical supplies.

During his time on the reservations, Montezuma became extremely concerned about the welfare of his people. He saw lack of education and the government's attitude that the Indian could not take care of himself as the major reasons for the "Indian condition." Under these circumstances, the Indian had little hope for a better life. Montezuma reasoned that in order to help his people, he needed to work towards healing their social wounds before he could hope to heal their physical ills.

After five years, Montezuma became disheartened and left his position as physician on the reservations. He served at Carlisle Indian School for two and one-half years then resigned from the Indian Service in 1896 to join Dr. Fenton B. Truck in his medical practice specializing in gastrointestinal disorders. He worked hard, but gaining wealth was not his main interest. Once he became a successful and respected Chicago physician, he began to speak out about conditions on the reservation. Although he had been making frequent speeches since his college days, he began to speak more often and with a stronger voice. He targeted the

Bureau of Indian Affairs as the cause of most of the problems on the reservation.

The United States government created the Bureau of Indian Affairs in an attempt to meet the needs of the American Indian population. In fact, the bureau did almost everything for the Indians and left them few responsibilities. Montezuma believed this government control prevented the Indians from providing for themselves and destroyed motivation and self-reliance. Montezuma wanted the same opportunities for Indian children as were available to other children. He wanted them to be educated, find jobs to support themselves, and survive in the modern world. He wanted the Indian to share in the benefits of civilization according to his own abilities, the same as white people.

In 1899, Dr. Montezuma began serving as physician to the Carlisle football team. Two years later, in 1901, while on the way to San Francisco with the team, he visited Fort McDowell, Arizona, home of the Yavapai Indians. There he found his cousins, the Dickens family. They told him of the fate of his family. His mother had been killed by an Indian scout as she searched for him and his sisters after the Pima attack. His two sisters had been taken to Mexico, where they died within a few years. His father had lived a few years after the tribe moved to the reservation. Dr. Montezuma maintained a relationship with his cousins on the reservation the rest of his life. He joined them in a fight for their rights and learned that reservation life offered a sense of community to the Indians and kept the tribe together.

Although he softened slightly in his opposition to reservation life, he still held strong views about the Indians' future. Dr. Montezuma spoke of his dreams for "The Indian of Tomorrow" in a speech he gave to the Illinois Woman's Press Association:

> . . . Surrounded as he has been by all manner of hindrances and misfortune, the Indian of tomorrow is living here and there, a few at least, in almost every northern and western state and territory, having risen above the circumstances which handicapped his people until he is one in civilization, in business and public affairs, with his pale-face brother . . . found in every profession, industry, and calling; educated, worldwise . . . His hopes lie in the possibility of

becoming a full man, and not that he may be made simply a "better Indian."

Throughout his life, Dr. Montezuma held the Bureau of Indian Affairs responsible for the ills of the reservation Indians brought on by idleness and lack of self-worth. He implored the United States government to release his people from captivity on the reservations by abolishing the Bureau of Indian Affairs. He also spoke out in favor of an organization that would represent all Indian tribes as one people. However, when the Society of American Indians was formed in 1911, Carlos Montezuma did not attend its first annual conference, in protest of the Bureau of Indian Affairs' involvement in the society. His speeches against the bureau began to reflect his desire to make the Society of American Indians a completely separate organization.

During this time, in 1913, Montezuma married Maria Keller, a German-speaking Rumanian.

By the time of the society's fourth annual conference in 1914, members of the press recognized Carlos Montezuma as "one of

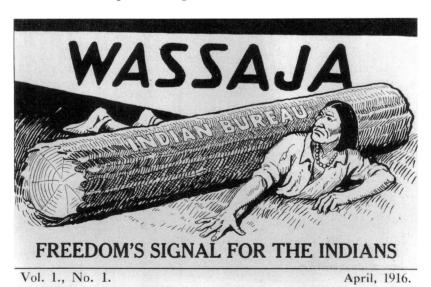

The Wassaja masthead *expressed Montezuma's strong feelings against the Bureau of Indian Affairs.* (Carlos Montezuma Collection, Arizona Collection, Arizona State University Libraries)

the most widely known Indians in the country." The next year, in a speech read before the Society of American Indians' Fifth Annual Conference at Lawrence, Kansas, on September 30, 1915, he said:

> The highest duty and greatest object, of the Society of American Indians, is to have a bill introduced in our next Congress to have the Indian Bureau abolished and to let the Indians go . . . We must act as one. In behalf of our people, with the spirit of Moses, I ask this,—THE UNITED STATES OF AMERICA,—"LET MY PEOPLE GO."

After this speech, the September 30 issue of the *Lawrence Daily Journal World* acknowledged Dr. Montezuma as "A splendid speaker—[who] would be called one on any rostrum between the oceans—on any subject he might elect to speak from."

The following May, as the Senate prepared to vote on an Indian Appropriations Conference report, Senator Jones of Washington read Dr. Montezuma's speech into the *Congressional Record* "in order to show the views of an educated full-blooded Indian with reference to the conduct of Indian affairs." Sadly, the speech received little attention from those in charge of funding the Bureau of Indian Affairs. By request from the floor, the last half of the speech with the request to "let my people go" was entered into the record without being read aloud.

As he continued his fight in 1916, Dr. Montezuma established a newspaper solely to carry his views concerning the Bureau of Indian Affairs. He called his monthly newspaper *Wassaja, Freedom's Signal for the Indian.* He accepted no advertising and supported the paper with his own money. Dr. Montezuma's strongest opinions appeared on the pages of *Wassaja.* He continued to speak out against the Bureau of Indian Affairs and drew attention to the organization of the Society of American Indians. Sometimes he supported the bureau's activities and sometimes he opposed them.

In 1922, Dr. Montezuma became ill. He had tuberculosis and, as a physician, he knew what the outcome would be. He revealed his failing health in the October 1922 issue of *Wassaja.* In the last issue, published November 1922, he continued his outcry against the Bureau of Indian Affairs. He titled his last article "The Indian Bureau—the Slaughter House of the Indian People."

In December of that year, Dr. Montezuma left Chicago. He boarded a train bound for Fort McDowell and his people, the Yavapai. He stopped in Phoenix to buy six woolen blankets and six comforters. He asked his relatives, the Dickens family, to build a brush shelter near their home. Back with his people, he rejected medical help and prepared to die as a Yavapai, in a simple brush shelter on a pile of blankets. With his wife, Maria, by his side, Carlos Montezuma died January 31, 1923, at three in the afternoon. He is buried at Fort McDowell.

Carlos Montezuma's life spanned little more than half a century, yet he witnessed near destruction of his people's culture. Knowing the old ways would never be again, he forged a place for himself in white America and gained the respect of both races. In doing so, he fought for the rights of his people. A year after his death, Congress passed the Indian Citizenship Act, making Indians citizens of the United States. The Bureau of Indian Affairs still exists, yet many Indians still live on reservations without many of the advantages the outside world has to offer. Others, however, have followed Montezuma's path by getting an education and establishing their place in the modern world.

RUTH HILLS WADSWORTH

Mescalero Apache Nurse
(c. 1886–1973)

In April 1917, the United States entered World War I, joining France and Britain in defense against the invading German forces. As American soldiers and sailors sailed to Europe, at war since 1914, American nurses volunteered their services. They were needed not only to care for the wounded, but also to provide general health care for American forces away from home. In addition, as the war devastated France, Red Cross nurses helped ease the suffering of the civilian population. Although the war effort encouraged more young women to enter nurse training, without careful organization, the growing demand for nurses abroad threatened to leave hospitals in the United States under-staffed.

Although American Indians were not citizens of the United States until Congress passed the Indian Citizenship Act in 1924, they were drafted into the military during World War I. Many volunteered, and as Indian men went to war, fighting for free-doms that were not extended to them, Indian women served as nurses. Having graduated from nursing school in 1911, Ruth

Hills's six years' professional experience made her a valuable candidate for overseas service. A Mescalero Apache, she claimed to be the first American Indian to serve as a Red Cross nurse overseas.

Ruth Hills was probably born near the Arizona-New Mexico-Mexican border in 1886. Her father's name was Dinero, a Spanish word that means money. Little is known about her mother. Hills had at least one brother, Poco Dinero, named after his father. *Poco* means little. Poco Dinero later became known as "Pinero" because the Apache, as well as other tribes, have trouble pronouncing the English letter "D."

Ruth Hills's Mescalero Apache heritage can be traced only through her brother. Pinero was born near Monterrey, Mexico. However, he is known to have ridden with Geronimo on raids and later became an Indian Scout under General Miles. Although his parents could have been of some other tribe, they made their home with the Mescalero Apache. Therefore, Ruth and Pinero are considered to be Mescalero Apache.

The Mescalero, like the other bands of Apache Indians, including the Jicarilla, Mimbreno, Mogollon, Chiricahua, Tonto, Coyotero, and Pinaleno, constantly moved in search of food. At home in the desert as well as in the rugged mountains of Arizona, New Mexico, and Mexico, Apache could find food and water in areas where others perished. Most of these Apache bands ate mescal, a member of the agave plant family sometimes called century plant. The name Mescalero, refers to the use of this desert plant as food. Apache women placed this large artichoke-like cactus in a pit of hot coals and covered it with damp grass and earth. After baking it for twenty-four hours, they ate the large leaves immediately and sliced the heart to be dried for later use.

The Mescalero acquired horses and guns by raiding other tribes and Mexican settlements. This allowed them to replenish their forces after battle and fight again. Along with other bands of southern Apache, the Mescalero opposed relocation to the reservation to the bitter end. Wise warriors, the Apache only fought battles they could win. Unless they had the advantage, they fled without fighting.

In 1886, under the command of General Miles, the United States Cavalry sought to round up the last of the Southwest Indians, mostly Apache, and force them onto reservations. In an effort to avoid capture, the Apache broke into small bands and scattered, hiding their camps in the rugged terrain of the Southwest.

Dinero's family, including his three-week-old sister, belonged to a small band of Mescaleros camped near the Mexican border. When the soldiers attacked, the Mescaleros fled into Mexico, as was their custom. After the battle quieted and the dust had settled, the soldiers found the baby had been accidentally left behind in the abandoned camp. They took her to the nearby Hills ranch.

That day, towards the end of July 1886, the soldiers effectively transformed the Apache infant's life. The Hills family named the tiny Apache girl Ruth and raised her as their own.

When the last Apache chief, Geronimo, surrendered, peace came to Indian Territory. With their leader on his way to prison

HOTEL DIEU. SANITARUM OF THE SISTERS OF CHARITY.

The Hotel Dieu in El Paso at the time Ruth Hills Wadsworth attended nursing school there. (El Paso County Historical Society)

in Florida, Ruth's fellow tribesmen were relocated to reservations. They left behind the lifestyle they had inherited from past generations. Few Apache of this generation would accept the new way and even fewer would become educated. For the Mescalero Apache, bewildered by the loss of freedom and unwelcome outside the boundaries of the reservation, time stood still.

With no knowledge of modern medicine or surgery, the Apache relied on their beliefs in the supernatural powers of the medicine man to heal their wounds and cure their illnesses. Beating a drum, the medicine man chanted and danced around his patient. When this ritual failed to cure the patient, the medicine man usually looked for someone to blame. He usually chose an old woman to accuse of casting an evil spell. This usually caused a fight between the family of the patient and that of the accused. In the chaos, the medicine man's power went unchallenged.

While members of her tribe clung to the lifestyle of the past, Ruth went to school with the white children in the area. After her general education, she completed one year of college before entering nursing school. Although she is said to have attended Vassar, the college has been unable to confirm her enrollment there.

Ruth attended nursing school at the prestigious Hotel Dieu School of Nursing in El Paso, Texas, recognized by medical professionals as the finest in the Southwest and one of the best in the country. The nursing school was established in 1898 to meet the nursing needs of the expanding Hotel Dieu Hospital. Ruth Hills enrolled in 1908 at the age of twenty-two. After a two-month probation period, she received $5 a month plus room, board, laundry, and sick care during her three-year course of study. At that time, student nurses lived on the top floor of the five-story Hotel Dieu Hospital. Ruth graduated in 1911. At age twenty-five, she began her career as a private-duty nurse.

In choosing her profession, Ruth followed in the footsteps of her ancestors. Among her people (and most other tribes), medicine women held a place of honor, and women looked on the opportunity to learn tribal medicine as a privilege. The Canadian Sisters of Charity began teaching Indian women basic nursing skills in the early-eighteenth century. By the twentieth century, Indian women had built a reputation for possessing qualities and attitudes well suited to the nursing profession. Lavinia L. Dock, R.N., secretary of the International Council of Nurses, wrote in *A History of Nursing* in 1912 that "The Indian woman has qualities that fit her excellently for the nurse's calling. Her nerves are under perfect control, and she is quite gentle. In cases that demand calmness and quick action she never fails, nor is she ever terrified by the sights and sounds of hospital life."

Carlisle (the Pennsylvania boarding school where Indian children were educated in the nineteenth century) soon recognized the opportunities for Indian women in nursing. According to an article in *The Red Man* (a monthly magazine written by Indians and published by the Carlisle Indian Press) in 1910, the school added a nursing course to its curriculum.

Some who took the nursing course did not seek a career outside the home. However, their families benefited from their training. Zippa Skenandore wrote in 1912,

> I think nursing is the grandest thing for girls to know, how to take care of the sick in their own family or in others. I know I never regretted that I did learn nursing . . . I have a family of seven to take care of. It is a great help to me.

Betty Wind Driven, another Indian nurse wrote, "I like nursing in all its branches, and my opinion of it for the Indian girls is that they are gifted with the art of nursing."

Ruth Hills, however, did not let household duties interfere with her nursing career. By the time the United States entered World War I, Ruth had married Clarence Raymond Wadsworth. According to Jane A. Delano, R.N., being married during World War I would have eliminated Ruth from military nursing service. Delano wrote in *The American Journal of Nursing*, October 1918, that "as yet, the Surgeon General has not been willing to accept married nurses for service in Military hospitals either in this country or abroad." However, the Surgeon General assigned the Red Cross the duty of organizing the distribution of the nation's nurses. It tackled the challenge of meeting the demand for 25,000 nurses to serve overseas without leaving America short of nursing care. In order to meet the need abroad, the Red Cross held to its own rules and allowed married nurses to serve in France as long as they did not have husbands serving there. Under these guidelines, Ruth became a Red Cross nurse assigned to duty in France.

In France, Red Cross nurses worked with the civilian population and in temporary assignments caring for American soldiers brought to French hospitals, as they were needed to help alleviate the shortage of nurses. Language presented a problem for those who did not speak French. The Red Cross used Americans who spoke fluent French as nurses' aids to bridge the language barrier between American nurses and French hospital personnel.

Hills was one of the Red Cross nurses who made a major contribution to the devastated civilian population of France. As the German armies advanced, French women and children fled, leaving their homes to seek safety away from the front. In the chaos, children found themselves separated from their parents. According to the *Literary Digest,* September 1918, "The number of children needing assistance . . . has now reached a stupendous total of 600,000 . . . of those, the French Government is caring for about 400,000. The rest of the work must be done by Americans (American Red Cross)." A shortage of doctors made life even more difficult for the French women and children. In many districts, three or four doctors (too old to go to war) tried to carry the patient load a hundred or more doctors had borne before the war. Illness and flu epidemics accompanied the refugees wherever they went. As the devastation grew, the need for Red Cross nurses increased.

In 1918, at the time of the signing of the armistice, 342 graduate nurses served in France. The end of the war, however, did not end the demand for nurses in France. American troops stayed to rebuild the war-torn nation, and Ruth Hill may have been one of the American nurses who continued caring for the general health of the troops and the wounded. The nurses also worked to restore normal life for the civilian population.

Sometime after the war, Ruth returned to her people and the land of her birth. According to records at the Mescalero Apache

Tribe in New Mexico, ". . . when she returned from Europe she remained on the Mescalero reservation for a while."

During this time, Ruth traced her brother Pinero's whereabouts to Indiahoma, Oklahoma. According to the account given in the *Hobart Democrat Chief*, August 4, 1925, "She went to the Mescalero Agency . . . and there got word of her brother, Pinero, of whom she had formerly known nothing." She traveled to Oklahoma to see him and "the contrast between the old Indian, Pinero, with his broken English and native habits and his full-blood sister . . . with her perfect English and refined manner was quite striking."

After spending some time on the Mescalero reservation, Ruth and her husband Clarence moved to Randsburg, California, a small mining town in the Mojave Desert. There Ruth continued her career as a nurse. Clarence died in 1946 and Ruth ended her fifty-year nursing career at the age of seventy-five, retiring in 1961. Suffering from cardiovascular disease, she moved to the Magnolia Gardens Convalescent Hospital in Granada Hills, California, about five years before her death in December 1973.

Ruth Hills Wadsworth, like many ordinary Americans, served this country by meeting its humanitarian needs. Early in her career, Ruth worked in a foreign country to preserve freedom that was denied to her own people in their homeland. Receiving little recognition, she continued her career until her own health failed. Although her name has all but disappeared from public record, she made a contribution to society. Somewhere, someone may still remember dark eyes filled with compassion, a cool hand on a feverish brow, and gentle words that soothed a frightened heart.

CHIEF TWO MOON MERIDAS

Pueblo/Blackfoot Herbalist
(1888–1933)

Congress passed patent legislation in 1793 that allowed people to file for the exclusive right to sell a certain product. Under this law, inventors and manufacturers "patented" their products so no one else could make and sell another product just like theirs. To acquire a patent, a description of the product had to be filed with the patent office. Since most medicine makers did not want to reveal their formulas, they applied for patents on the shape of the bottle and the label. Labels contained the product name, an identifying symbol or picture, and, usually, highly exaggerated claims for cure. Thus, the formulas for early "patent medicines" were not protected by law but held secret. Without regulations and control, most of these medicines ranged from worthless to harmful. Some contained powerful and dangerous narcotics such as cocaine, opium, and morphine, and most had a high alcohol content.

Indian remedies became very popular about this time. Many people were convinced that plants and herbs found only in North America could cure disease. And, they thought the American

Indians knew the secret formulas. So, the patent medicine makers jumped on the bandwagon, and junk medicine with Indian-sounding names became very popular. By 1904, patent medicine had become a $74.5 million business and had earned a shady reputation.

Then in 1906, Congress passed the Pure Food and Drug Act, which required narcotic ingredients to be listed on the labels of proprietary (patent) medicines and prohibited the use of outrageous, misleading claims. Further controls were passed in the Harrison Narcotic Act of 1914, which limited the amounts of opium, heroin, morphine, and cocaine allowed in over-the-counter drugs (sold without prescriptions).

By the time Chief Two Moon Meridas and his wife established the Two Moon Herb Co. in Waterbury, Connecticut, these controls were in place. His medicines contained none of the restricted narcotic substances. As in the old days, alcohol content made some medicines popular; however, only one of Chief Two Moon's herbal medicines contained a significant amount of alcohol. His Cough Elixir featured a 25 percent alcohol base.

One belief held steadfast from the heyday of uncontrolled patent medicines: that cures for diseases could be found in the plants and herbs of North America and that American Indians knew the secret formulas.

Born Chico Colon Meridan on August 29, 1888 in South Dakota, Chief Two Moon claimed descent from two Indian tribes, the Blackfoot and Pueblo. His father was Chico Colon Meridan. He took the name Two Moon from his mother, Mary Tumoon. He later changed his last name to Meridas.

Little is known about Chief Two Moon's early life. He is said to have learned about herbs and roots when he lived on a reservation in South Dakota as a boy. He left the reservation when he was twelve and joined a carnival troupe. He traveled the country proclaiming the virtues of herbs and roots in the treatment of human ills.

Chief Two Moon Meridas (Courtesy Thomas J. Fillius and Loretta R. Nugent)

In 1914, he married Helen Gertrude Nugent in Brooklyn, New York. Two Moon and Helen sold herbal potions on the street corners of Philadelphia and New York before they moved to the Graf rooming house on Griggs Street in Waterbury, Connecticut. The couple continued selling herbal medicines in Waterbury.

During the severe flu epidemic of 1918, all the users of Chief Two Moon's herbal medicine survived. Word began to spread and fame followed. By 1921, having more business than he could efficiently conduct from the rooming house, Chief Two Moon moved to a house-and-store combination on Wales Street.

His "Bitter Oil—the Wonder Tonic" soon became his most popular medicine. Meridas advertised Bitter Oil as a "miracle medicine [that] removes all internal poisons, thus relieving constipation, gastric conditions, sick headache, biliousness, kidney and bladder troubles, etc. Consistent use will soon put vigor and vitality into any run-down system." Bitter Oil contained mineral oil, tincture of aloes, and compound tincture of gentian. These ingredients are common. Mineral oil is a colorless and tasteless petroleum product used as a laxative. Aloe is a bitter laxative made from the juice of certain aloe leaves. Gentian is a bitter root used as a gastrointestinal tonic.

Before long, leading drugstores carried Bitter Oil along with Chief Two Moon Herb Co.'s other products. Displays of Chief Two Moon products filled storefront windows with full-color posters and lifesize stand-up cutouts of the chief in full Indian attire, including a war bonnet. Meridas also marketed his products through traveling salesmen or direct from the company by mail order.

Chief Two Moon received many letters praising the popularity of his products. In 1925, James A. Hetherington, a New York pharmacist, wrote Chief Two Moon saying, "We have been handling Chief Two Moon Bitter Oil for the past two years and found it to be one of our most popular as well as profitable sellers." About the same time, the Hindle Drug Stores, Inc. of Bridgeport, Connecticut, wrote a similar testimonial: "Due to . . . the beneficial results obtained by customers who use it [Chief Two Moon's Bitter Oil] regularly, we find our sales of same to be very gratifying. Two gross a month, and are steadily increasing as the Oil becomes better known."

Chief Two Moon advertised in newspapers across the country, as did his competitors. In fact, the newspaper business and patent medicine companies formed a mutually beneficial alliance. The major source of revenue for the early newspapers was from patent medicine advertising. In turn, advertising dramatically increased sales of patent medicines. As business increased, the Chief Two Moon Herb Co. expanded to include a corps of salesmen transported by busses, plus delivery trucks, a fleet of ten Lincoln automobiles, and an airplane. The company soon outgrew the house on Wales Street and Meridas built a laboratory. The building that housed the Two Moon Herb Co. laboratory still stands today on Main Street in Waterbury, Connecticut.

Chief Two Moon's All Herb medicines soon were readily available, and people seeking relief from ailments flocked to see Meridas in person. Although they came to him, Two Moon did not refer to these people as patients: He was a medicine man, not a licensed doctor. These "out-of-town visitors" came from all areas of the northeastern United States. The cars parked along the street outside his home-office bore license plates from New York, New Jersey, Maine, Rhode Island, Massachusetts, Vermont, New Hampshire, and Pennsylvania.

Meridas sometimes entertained his guests with sleight of hand and fortune telling. Some said he was clairvoyant and that "his eyes seemed to bore into you." Many of his clients thought he used supernatural powers to diagnose their ills. A visitor from Warren, Ohio, wrote that "his supernatural power of discerning ailments of the human body and prescribing relief places him at once in the front ranks of benefactors of his brother man."

Satisfied customers wrote letters praising Two Moon products. J. S. Braren, pastor of St. Mark's Evangelical Lutheran Church in Jamaica, New York wrote:

> Having arrived in the critical age of the middle fifties . . . I found myself lacking in vitality . . . Then I gave myself into your skillful care and for three months followed your regime as faithfully as possible. Now after the interval of four months I can say . . . I have

enjoyed perfect health without even becoming the victim of a single winter cold; I have carried on my work with unusual vigor and success . . . I certainly attribute this physical and mental alertness to the splendid treatment received at the hands of Chief Two Moon Meridas . . .

Two Moon Meridas did not charge a fee for listening to complaints or recommending specific herbal medicines. He only charged for the herbal medicines. The prepackaged products, including Bitter Oil, were available in three sizes. A small (8-oz.) bottle sold for $1.00, a medium (12-oz.) bottle sold for $1.25, and a large (16-oz.) bottle sold for $1.50. A custom mixture of herbs from big bins he kept in his consultation room sold for $5 a bag.

The Chief Two Moon Herb Co. order blank listed several prepackaged herbal medicines, including All Herb Rheumatism Relief, All Herb Stomach Relief, All Herb Asthma Relief, All Herb Female Tonic Relief, All Herb Liver Relief, All Herb Kidney Relief,

A Chief Two Moon Herb Co. delivery truck   (Courtesy Thomas J. Fillius and Loretta R. Nugent)

All Herb Tonic (Builder) Relief, Skin Cream, Cough Elixir, Pile Ointment, Liniment, and Household Ointment.

Each medicine contained a variety of herbs. His Stomach Tea, for example, contained thirteen herbs: tinnevelly senna, coriander seed, gentian root, juniper berries, centaury, calamus root, buckthorn bark, Jamaica ginger, cascara sagrada, pale rose buds, anise seed, lavender flowers, and fennel seed.

No one knows the exact source of Chief Two Moon's formulas. In many cases they were similar to medications being used by medical doctors at the time. According to Varro E. Tyler, Lily Distinguished Professor of Pharmacognosy (natural medicine) at the School of Pharmacy and Pharmacal Sciences at Purdue University, Two Moon's formulas "drew upon the conventional medical wisdom of the period and, in many cases, incorporated the same remedies, both botanical and chemical, that would have been utilized for the same conditions by practitioners of orthodox medicine. The source is unknown but probably drew on the numerous formularies and dispensatories of the early twentieth century."

About 1929, the Chief Two Moon Herb Co. established a branch business on Atlantic City's famous boardwalk. Meridas hired a Sioux chief, William Spotted Crow, and his family to operate the Indian Temple. The store sold Chief Two Moon All Herb medicines as well as Indian curios. Atlantic City officials welcomed the chief and presented him with the keys to the city. However, the Atlantic City Chamber of Commerce denied Chief Two Moon permission to do business in Atlantic City. This foiled any plans Chief Two Moon may have had to move his headquarters from Waterbury to Atlantic City.

Chief Two Moon remained in the small town of Waterbury and continued to charge low fees for his herbal medicines. Still, profits from the sale of his products, mainly from Bitter Oil, made Two Moon Meridas a rich man.

Chief Two Moon is said to have spent his money on expensive clothes, furniture, and travel. He also gave freely to those in need, often insisting that his generosity remain a secret. The extent of his kindness was not known until his friends and beneficiaries came together after his death. Mr. James Courtney, a friend of the chief's and the proprietor of a market near the chief's home, told of more than 300 families in Waterbury who had received help from Meridas. They had received assistance in many forms, including food, clothing, rent, and heating fuel. One family received help for two years while the father was unemployed. In another case, Meridas paid for a child's surgery. In an open gesture of generosity, Chief Two Moon played Santa Claus at Christmastime. In 1929 he distributed 200 turkeys, 4 tons of coal, 12 pairs of shoes, 200 dolls, and 100 baskets filled with food, fruit, and candy to needy families in Waterbury. "What he spent in ten years for charity," said Courtney, "was so high in the thousands that it would make an unbelievable total . . . Rent, fuel, clothes, doctor bills—he paid for anything and everything he was asked to by the poor."

Two Moon Meridas also extended his generosity to the impoverished Indians on the Pine Ridge Reservation in South Dakota. He visited the Oglala Sioux, one of the seven divisions of the Sioux Nation, in 1929. During his visit, Meridas tended to the ills of the Indians and bought them some cattle. He gave the chiefs of the Sioux tribe $500 in order to conduct ceremonies and they awarded him the title of "honorary chief" and "friend of the Indians." While visiting the Pine Ridge Reservation, Chief Two Moon realized that many of the older Sioux had stomach complaints and could benefit from his Bitter Oil product. After returning to Waterbury, he sent a large shipment to the postmaster at Pine Ridge to be distributed to the Indians. After receiving permission from the Commissioner of Indian Affairs, the postmaster distributed the medicine to the Indians.

In August 1930, Meridas again traveled to South Dakota. This time he contributed $1,000 to the Oglala and in return for his generosity was made a chief in a tribal ceremony.

After the ceremony was conducted on the Pine Ridge Reservation, Two Moon Meridas received an official document proclaiming him chief of all the Sioux. The body of the document, later printed in the *Waterbury Evening Democrat* on October 20, 1932, reads in part as follows:

. . . Chief Two Moon Meridas, an Indian Medicine Man of Waterbury, Connecticut, is hereby formally declared a member of the Oglala Sioux Nation; with all adequate and appropriate ceremony for such an occasion, he is made a Chief of the Oglala Sioux. That henceforth he shall be recognized as a true representative of the Sioux Nation of Indians and that he is duly authorized and empowered to represent the Sioux Indians in the manner and power usually invested in our Chiefs: that he is the sponsor and Honorary President of the Pine Ridge Sioux Rodeo, an annual event on the Pine Ridge reservation. Further, that he is deserving of and is entitled to all respect, honor, and courtesy which is customarily accorded an Indian Chieftain of this Nation.

That same day, the Sioux also signed papers making Chief Two Moon a good-will ambassador to any European sovereign power he might visit during his planned European trip.

In the fall of 1930, Chief Two Moon and his wife traveled to Europe where they had a private audience with Pope Pius XI. The Vatican newspaper referred to Chief Two Moon as the "leader of the Indians." While in Rome, Chief Two Moon received recognition from Italian surgeons and physicians as the "great medicine man from America." They also praised his ability to diagnose illnesses.

Although Meridas received extensive praise for his abilities and herbal medicines at home and abroad, there were those who thought he was a quack selling something akin to snake oil. Herbal medicine in the United States has always been viewed with far more skepticism than in Europe. According to Professor Norman R. Farnsworth, an expert in natural medicines at the University of Illinois at Chicago, "We have no history of it like in England or in Germany. We have Indian medicine men, and nobody thinks much of them." Today, however, modern scientists are taking a serious look at plant medicine as they search the world's rainforest for cures for cancer and AIDS. The discovery that the leaves of a Madagascan periwinkle plant contain a powerful drug successfully used for treating childhood leukemia brings to mind the possibility that other plants might have the potential to fight disease.

After Meridas returned from Europe, an employee filed suit against him as part of a wage dispute. The suit also questioned the propriety of Meridas's relationship with the Sioux. In response, Chief Two Moon spared no expense in bringing twenty-six Sioux chiefs to Waterbury to speak on his behalf. He posted a $1,000 bond for each Indian who left the reservation and provided bus transportation and lavish entertainment for the group at his Beacon Valley estate.

After the Sioux chiefs gave their depositions, but before the lawsuit was settled, Chief Two Moon began having pains in his stomach. After a brief illness, Chief Two Moon died at his home on November 2, 1933. An autopsy revealed a ruptured vein in his thorax (the body cavity that contains the heart and lungs) and cirrhosis of the liver. Although this disease is commonly caused by excessive drinking, none of Chief Two Moon's friends recalled ever seeing him drunk. The possibility that some of the herbal medicines he took damaged his liver was considered. An examination of the ingredients in his formulas failed to reveal a likely cause of the liver damage. Years later, however, a report surfaced that Meridas may have drunk a bottle of champagne each morning.

Chief Two Moon Meridas was buried in Hillside Cemetery in Roslyn, Pennsylvania. His wife, Helen Nugent Meridas, continued the Two Moon Herb Co. until she retired and closed the fifty-year-old business in 1969.

The American Institute of the History of Pharmacy recognized Chief Two Moon as "a name to be recorded in the history of patent medicine in America." Often called a "modern miracle man," Two Moon himself never claimed to have performed a healing miracle; however, thousands of his "out of town visitors" insisted that he cure them when medical science had failed. Although attempts to discredit Chief Two Moon have been made by some, he is long remembered as a caring and generous man by most of those who knew him. Raymond Bergamo worked as Chief Two Moon's chauffeur in 1928. He was seventeen at the time. Fifty-five years later, in 1983, Bergamo remembered Two Moon as being "generous and easy to work for . . . a hard worker and a good man."

HERBERT BURWELL FOWLER

Santee Sioux Psychiatrist (1919–77)

In the early 1800s, as army physicians on military posts began vaccinating the members of nearby tribes, deaths from smallpox began to decline. However, another, more vicious threat had accompanied the explorers, traders, and settlers into Indian lands. Unlike smallpox, which took its victims within a few days, alcohol brought suffering that continued generation after generation. Statistics indicate that on average, the number of alcohol-related deaths on reservations is three to four times higher than outside. Through alcohol addiction, the consequences of drunken behavior, depression, and serious health problems plague the adult Indian population. In addition, when pregnant women drink, the alcohol consumed by the mother silently attacks her unborn child. As a result, alcohol's tiny, innocent victims are born with birth defects or inherited alcoholism.

Until the mid-1900s, although some people joked about Indians and drunkenness, outsiders paid little attention as long as the problem remained on the reservation. Some tribal leaders tried to ban the sale of alcohol on their reservations, but often their efforts

failed. This devastating problem received no professional attention until the last half of the twentieth century. Genetic psychiatrist Dr. Herbert Burwell Fowler was one of the first health care
professionals to concentrate on the alcohol problem. Through his
efforts, Indians began to receive mental health care and alcohol
treatment on the reservations. For his work in this area, he received international acclaim.

Herbert Burwell Fowler, one-quarter Santee Sioux, was born
April 14, 1919, in Cheyenne, Wyoming. Named after his father,
Herbert B. Fowler Sr., his Santee Sioux ancestry was through his
mother, Mary Eastman Fowler.

The Santee are the eastern division of the Dakota (also called
Sioux) Indians. They call themselves Oceti Sakowin, which means
seven council fires, because the tribe has seven political divisions.
Three of these, the Mdewakanton, Siseton, and Wahpeton, are
Eastern Dakota, known as the Santee and sometimes called the
Santee Sioux. The descendants of the Santee Sioux live in North
and South Dakota, Minnesota, Montana, and the Canadian prov-
inces of Alberta and Saskatchewan. Herbert Fowler spent a portion of his youth in the Pine Ridge area of North Dakota.

His grandfather, Charles Eastman, one of the first American
Indians to become a physician, graduated from medical school at
Boston University in 1890. After receiving his medical degree, Dr.
Eastman accepted a position with the Bureau of Indian Affairs'
Indian Health Service (IHS) on the Pine Ridge Reservation in
South Dakota. A few months later, in December 1890, the United
States Army attacked the Sioux at Wounded Knee Creek on the
Pine Ridge Reservation. In his capacity as IHS physician, Dr.
Eastman treated the wounded Indians. Historians record this
famous Battle of Wounded Knee as the last major armed conflict
between federal troops and American Indians. Dr. Eastman
served on the Pine Ridge Reservation until 1893, then resigned his
position to enter private practice in St. Paul, Minnesota. He returned to IHS as agency physician at the Crow Creek Reservation

in South Dakota in 1900. Dr. Eastman continued his medical career and became well-known for his contribution to society and involvement in Indian affairs.

Herbert Fowler followed his grandfather into the medical profession. After graduating from high school, probably in Cheyenne, Wyoming, he attended the University of Wyoming and received a bachelor of science in 1942. He continued his education at the University of Michigan, where he earned a degree in medicine and surgery in 1946.

After completing his internship at Harper Hospital in Detroit, Michigan, Dr. Fowler became a resident physician at the University of Utah College of Medicine in Salt Lake City.

During that time, he traveled to Europe to study various psychiatric installations for the National Institute of Mental Health. As Dr. Fowler established himself in the field of psychiatry he became one of eight Native American psychiatrists in the United States. He specialized in genetic psychiatry, which studies inheritance patterns in mental illness. While treating his patients, he studied their family histories to determine if other family members had suffered similar mental problems. Genetic psychiatry research also seeks answers to questions such as: Are certain mental illnesses passed from parent to child? Are certain illnesses more likely to be inherited by one gender? Are some illnesses more likely to afflict people of American Indian descent (or some other ethnic background)?

Throughout his life, Dr. Fowler gave special attention to the mental-health needs of American Indians. In fact, Dr. Fowler became well known in the United States for his research, as well as for mental health and alcohol treatment programs for Indians.

Although the rate of alcohol use varies from tribe to tribe, statistics indicate that more than one-third of all American Indian deaths are alcohol-related. This includes deaths from suicide, homicide, and accidental injuries, in addition to the health hazards of alcoholism (cirrhosis of the liver and damage to other vital organs).

For many years most people thought that Indians simply "couldn't hold their liquor." In other words, something about the

Herbert Fowler (courtesy of Reed Fowler)

Indian's metabolism that regulated the speed at which alcohol entered the blood stream worsened the effects of alcohol. However, some recent studies have concluded that the reason for so much alcoholism among Native Americans stems from emotional stress resulting from the loss of culture, tradition, and religion. In addition, as the American Indians are encouraged to seek a place in modern society, many are overwhelmed as they try to meet the demands of two cultures. In 1995, Senator Ben Nighthorse Campbell, an American Indian from Colorado, explained it this way:

> Indian kids have it tougher (than any other young people) because they not only have to face all the (everyday) challenges of survival, but they're also caught between two cultures. They have to not only try to learn from the elders, the old ones, the traditional values that have been handed down father-to-son and mother-to-daughter, but they also have to learn to live in twentieth century America and how to become leaders.

Western traits, such as aggressiveness in seeking wealth, the desire to obtain more personal property, and arguing loudly to settle disputes, clash with the traditional values of most tribes. These include having a cooperative spirit, sharing property, and feeling no need to make plans or commitments for the future. Having a value system conflicting with the majority in American society, many Indians find the path between these two worlds difficult to follow. Diane Glancy (of Cherokee descent) wrote an essay explaining her view of what it means to be an American Indian—past and present. She wrote that those who survive "have legs that walk between the noise of traffic and the silence of the prairie . . ." She went on to say, "I can dream and imagine the good road ahead, but I also need the discipline to set goals and strive to achieve them. Vision and work. The sense of being a real person in this world-that-is."

Studies have shown that squeezed between the past and present, American Indians display a lower level of self-esteem than any other ethnic group in the United States. Forced to live between two worlds, many American Indians experience a sense of powerlessness and hopelessness that creates emotional stress. Those who seek to relieve stress with alcohol only add to the existing mental or emotional problem.

Dr. Fowler believed that treatment of mental illness and alcoholism among the Indians must be culturally oriented to be effective. In other words, in order to treat American Indian patients, the health care worker must understand and respect the cultural tradition that is the heritage of his or her patient.

In 1958, in an attempt to fulfill this need, Dr. Fowler established the first mental health clinic on an Indian reservation. He served as director of this clinic, on the Ute Indian Reservation at Fort Duchesne, Utah, for six years. While still associated with the Ute Mental Health Clinic, Dr. Fowler took on added responsibility as director of mental health education for the University of Utah's College of Medicine. Serving in this capacity from 1962 to 1970, his responsibilities included overseeing mental health programs in six western states.

As his concept of combining culture with psychiatry spread, Dr. Fowler acted as a psychiatric consultant to many organizational and tribal groups, including the Utah State Hospital, the U.S. Peace Corps, the Wyoming State Hospital, and several Veterans Administration hospitals. He also served as associate professor of psychiatry at Michigan State Medical School and as administrator of the state hospital there. He was a member of the Indian Task Force of the Academy of Child Psychiatry, the Committee on Indian Affairs for the American Psychiatry Association, and the Oregon representative of the minority section of the American Association of Medical Colleges. Alaskan Native problems drew Dr. Fowler's interest and he visited Alaska on many speaking and consulting tours.

In 1975, Dr. Fowler moved to Portland, Oregon where he accepted a position as director of the Whitecloud Center at the University of Oregon Health Sciences Center. The National Tribal Chairmen's Association established the center with a $5 million grant from the National Institute of Mental Health. The research center developed mental-health treatment programs for American Indians and Native Alaskans, and established branch centers in Alaska, South Dakota, Oklahoma, and the Southwest.

By this time, Dr. Fowler had received international recognition. He was well-known in Russia for his extensive work in genetic psychiatry and his writings in psychotherapy. In November 1976, Dr. Fowler received a telegram from Vladimir Kirillin, chairman of the Soviet Committee on Science and Technology. The telegram confirmed the news Dr. Fowler had heard a few days earlier while in Washington, D.C., on business. He had been selected to receive the Lenin Prize in science. According to an article in the *Oregonian*, a Portland, Oregon, newspaper, Dr. Fowler was "the first American Indian to receive the Lenin Prize Laureate in science." In naming Dr. Fowler as the recipient of this award, the Soviet Union recognized Dr. Fowler for a number of his accomplishments. These accomplishments included his methods of administering a large state hospital in Michigan, his extensive research in genetic psychology, and his work at the Whitecloud Center.

Notification of winning the Lenin Prize came as a complete surprise to Dr. Fowler. He said in an interview the following Thursday, "It's the last thing in the world I expected. I knew there was such a prize but I didn't know much about it."

Lenin Prizes were awarded annually by the Soviet Union for outstanding achievements in science, literature, architecture, and cinema. According to the telegram, Dr. Fowler was to go to the Soviet Union May 15, 1977, to be honored at the Supreme Soviet Presidium in Moscow. Along with the honor, the prize included a $50,000 honorarium and a speaking tour of Soviet scientific centers.

Dr. Fowler and his wife Julia looked forward to the event and made plans to travel to Moscow. Unfortunately, Dr. Fowler suffered a massive cerebral hematoma (brain hemorrhage) and died at his home in Portland, Oregon, January 2, 1977. He would have been fifty-eight that April. He is survived by his wife and seven children.

A pioneer in mental health research, Dr. Fowler dedicated himself to healing the psychological ills of his people. Among the first professionals to attempt to relieve the devastating effects of alcohol on American Indians, Dr. Fowler began work that others must complete. Although strides have been made in treating alcoholism on reservations, American Indians still suffer greatly from its ill effects. Still, much credit goes to Dr. Fowler for seeing the need and beginning the work that brought him international recognition. Without doubt, Dr. Fowler lived up to the Santee Sioux name of his grandfather, Ohiyesa, "The Victor" or "Winner."

LORETTA SNYDER HELLE

Eskimo Physician
(1930–   )

As with other North American Indians, contact with Europeans influenced Eskimo culture. In the early eighteenth century, explorers came to northern Alaska in search of a Northwest Passage. Their reports of whale sightings brought whalers to the area. Some whalers settled in Alaska and married local women. Missionaries soon followed.

The missionaries came to stay permanently, seeking to convert the indigenous people to Christianity. They settled into the community, opened schools, and offered medical services along with Christian ethics. Methodist missionaries established a hospital in Nome, Alaska. The missionaries soon gained the trust of the Inupiat Eskimos. As a result, the Inupiats lost faith in the traditional medicine man and sought modern medical treatment.

Although Dr. Loretta Snyder Helle, a twentieth-century Eskimo from Nome, knows little about traditional medicine, she suspects "there may have been throw backs to Eskimo culture" among the elders in Nome when she was a child. Dr. Helle, however, grew up in the Methodist church and went to modern doctors at the

Methodist hospital for her medical care. She says that she might have come by her desire to be a doctor naturally since her great-grandfather was a medicine man.

One of five children, Loretta Snyder Helle was born on September 13, 1930, in Nome, Alaska. Her father, Roy Snyder, was half Inupiat and worked as a mechanic. Her mother, Anna Nelson Snyder, also half Inupiat, taught at the local Bureau of Indian Affairs school until the birth of their second child.

Eskimo is a foreign term to the Indians of the North. It means "eaters of raw meat" and was used by the original inhabitants of eastern Canada to describe their culturally distinct neighbors. Europeans picked up the word and it stuck. The designation the indigenous people of the North use to refer to themselves can be translated as "real people," and has three variations: Inupiat, for the people of northern Alaska; Inuit, for the people of Greenland and Canada; and Yuit, for people native to southwestern Alaska and Siberia.

In the past, the Inupiat culture revolved around hunting, fishing, and food gathering. Living in the frozen North, the Inupiat hunted seals, walruses, whales, polar bears, and caribou. Having few resources, they used every part of the animals they killed. They ate the meat and fat, sometimes raw, as their name suggests, and other times boiled in a rich broth. With sinew thread and bone needles, they made clothing from the skins of seals, caribou, and polar bears. They also used skins to make tents and boat covers. Animal bones became weapons and tools.

Because the area still lacks industry, hunting and fishing continue to occupy an important part of life in the Far North. For this reason, the Inupiat continue to resist building roads between villages. They fear the resulting traffic would destroy their hunting grounds.

Loretta Snyder attended public school in Nome while most Eskimos went to the Bureau of Indian Affairs school. Her mother insisted that the Snyder children go to public schools despite the discrimination Eskimo children faced there. The Eskimo children were denied opportunity, discouraged, and sometimes humiliated. One incident occurred when Loretta was in first grade and her class went to the nurse's office to be weighed. "We were so poor that instead of felt soles, I had straw in my mukluks." Dr. Helle recalled. When she took off her mukluks to be weighed, some of the straw spilled on the rug. "Instead of the nurse cleaning it up, which is what I would do," Dr. Helle recalled, "she marched back down to the room and announced that whoever put the straw on the rug had to clean it up."

Trying to forget the humiliating experience, Loretta began to notice that good grades brought rewards and recognition from her teachers. With this encouragement, she worked hard at her studies and earned a reputation as a high achiever and a position near the top of her class. Her accomplishments helped her overcome the early incidents of racial discrimination.

At that time, in the 1930s and 1940s, people who lived in Alaska traveled by dogsled in winter (today they use snowmobiles). Summer prospectors came by boat to comb the beach for gold. After big storms, young Loretta sometimes found small nuggets as she walked along the beach.

With the exception of the summer prospectors, a small airfield brought the only contact with the outside world. "We were very isolated," Dr. Helle later remembered. "There were no roads going to Nome. I read an awful lot." Through her reading, young Loretta learned about the world. As she watched the small planes land and take off at the airfield, she thought the stewardess had the most glamorous job around. She decided she would be a stewardess someday so she could see the world she read about.

While in high school, Loretta made plans to go to nursing school in order to fulfill the nurse's training required in order to become a stewardess in the 1940s. Her plans changed when she suffered an attack of appendicitis and had to have her appendix removed. Her stay in the Methodist hospital gave her a firsthand look at what nurses actually did. As a result, Loretta lost interest in going to nursing school and becoming a stewardess. "I saw them (nurses) carrying bed pans around," she said, "And I decided I wanted to be a doctor."

After she recovered from surgery and returned to school, she told her math teacher, Max Bieberman, that she was thinking about becoming a doctor. Recognizing her potential, Bieberman encouraged her. "You can always shoot for the top," he said. "And if you can't make it you can always try for something lesser."

Loretta graduated with honors from Nome High School in 1948. As valedictorian, she received a scholarship to attend Washington State University at Pullman, Washington. The scholarship, offered to all valedictorians graduating from Alaska high schools, paid for living quarters for one school year. Loretta chose a private room in the freshman dorm.

Busy with her studies, Loretta allowed herself little time to think about Nome. Then one morning she opened her curtains to the sight of the campus blanketed in white. Seeing the snow brought on a severe attack of homesickness. A young girl who had never been away from her family and seldom away from home, she pulled her pillow over her head that night and sobbed. Climatic differences and cultural attitudes made life difficult for the small-town girl from the land of ice and snow. She didn't know anyone and felt lost among the 7,000 students attending Washington State that year. By her second year, she had adjusted to the Washington culture and weather and began to make friends. But a new problem arose. No longer on scholarship, she faced financial difficulties. Her father, proud of her success and courage in going away to school, wanted her to continue her education. He contacted the Bureau of Indian Affairs and requested a loan for Loretta's education. The agent in Nome asked Roy Snyder what his daughter was studying. When he learned that she was in pre-med, he suggested that if she were to change to nursing, the loan would probably be approved. The agent considered a medical education for a girl to be "money down the drain" and thought she would get married, have children, and never practice medicine. For this reason, the agent denied Snyder the loan.

Denial of the loan, however, did not stop Loretta Snyder from getting her education. She worked part time during the school year and full time in the summer. She applied for small scholarships called "book scholarships." Filling out the long forms netted between $20 and $50, and few students bothered to apply for these scholarships. This gave Loretta an advantage and helped ease her money problems.

Although able to scrape by with part-time and summer jobs, Loretta faced further discrimination. Women students were required to have two pre-med majors while men needed only one. Loretta majored in bacteriology and public health. She later said: "That served me well because I could work as a lab tech to earn money for medical school."

While in medical school at the University of Washington in Seattle, Loretta continued to face far more discrimination as a woman than as an Indian. Only 3 percent of medical school enrollment was open to women. In other words, in a class of 100 medical students, only three could be women. When called on in class, Loretta and her two women classmates were ridiculed if they did not know an answer. She later said, the women "just had to perform 110 percent instead of 100 percent."

Along with financial difficulties and discrimination, Loretta faced another challenge—she contracted tuberculosis. This disease was very common among Eskimos. In fact, other members of her family had suffered from the disease. Symptoms include fatigue, loss of weight and appetite, night sweats, fever, and persistent cough. Tuberculosis was a leading cause of death among all peoples until the discovery of antituberculous drugs in the 1940s. Even with antituberculous treatment, Loretta faced a lengthy recovery requiring extensive rest. In a weakened condition when she returned to the university, Loretta could not carry a full class load. As a result, it took her three years to complete her last two years of medical school.

During this time, she met her husband-to-be, James Helle, an oceanography student at the University of Washington. They were married in 1957.

By the time Loretta received her medical degree in 1958, she was expecting their first child. She gave birth to a boy that summer and moved to San Diego, California, where her husband took a position with Scripps Institute of Oceanography. Dr. Helle began her internship at San Diego County General, now known as UCSD (University of California at San Diego) Medical Center, in November of 1958. Upon finishing her internship the following May, Dr. Helle planned to do her residency in psychiatry. Unfortunately, there were no openings in psychiatric residency programs in the San Diego area. Like other Native American physicians, Dr. Helle saw the necessity to treat the whole pa-

Dr. Loretta Helle says this is the way her patients saw her—always casual.
(Courtesy of Olan Mills Studios and Loretta Helle)

tient—psychological as well as physical illnesses. She believes that in general practice, 50 percent of a doctor's work is in psychiatry.

From the time she decided to go to medical school, Dr. Helle planned to return to Nome and practice medicine among her own people. However, once she married, her plans changed. Her husband's career took the Helle family to a permanent home in San Diego.

By the time Dr. Helle completed her internship, the Helles had a second child. In order to meet the demands of her family and her career, Dr. Helle decided to forgo private practice and take a forty-hour-a-week job with the Public Health Service.

Along with caring for her family and pursuing her career, Dr. Helle has given much of her time to Indian programs, including the Southern California Alaskan Natives Association, California Rural Indian Health Project on the Palo Reservation near San Diego, and American Indians for Future and Tradition. She has also been active in civic and community organizations in the San Diego area.

After the death of an infant daughter in 1970, Dr. Helle found it too difficult to continue her work with the Public Health Service, where she worked mostly with women and children. She decided to establish her own practice in industrial medicine. In this practice, Dr. Helle worked with companies as a consultant. She evaluated health conditions at the companies and offered recommendations for improvement. This included concerns about health hazards in the workplace such as contaminated air, noise levels, proper protective equipment, and possible exposure to harmful chemicals or radiation. To help overcome her grief at the loss of her daughter, she also began studying law at night at this time. Although Dr. Helle had no intention of becoming a lawyer, she continued with her studies and graduated from the University of San Diego Law School in 1973.

Dr. Helle took an early retirement in 1985 but found she "couldn't stand retirement." While weighing the possibilities, she thought about "going back to work and earning more money," but instead joined the Peace Corps.

The United States government established the Peace Corps in 1961. This program sends American volunteers with experience in education, health care, agriculture, and rural and small business development to share their knowledge with the people of developing countries. Others are prepared to supply trained manpower to aid in construction and agriculture. Any United States citizen over the age of 18 may apply to volunteer for the Peace Corps. The tour of duty, after training, is two years. Volunteers receive a small allowance and work and live among the people as a part of the community.

Dr. Helle, who says she has "always been a Christian," felt that "the Lord led her that way." She served as a Peace Corps physician for two years, from 1985 to 1987, because she "wanted to give something to people who don't have much." She went to the Dominican Republic, a small country that borders Haiti on the island of Hispaniola in the Caribbean. The island lies between Cuba and Puerto Rico off the coast of Mexico. While in the Dominican Republic, Dr. Helle worked with a local doctor in a rural clinic. In the mornings, she accompanied him into the mountains, where she saw patients, mostly children. In the afternoons she gave talks on community health concerns, which included child care, sanitation, and nutrition.

Dr. Helle treasures her experience with the Peace Corps and considers it one of the highlights of her career. She says she gained insight while serving in the Dominican Republic, "You really get to know yourself and what you are capable of doing, and what is beyond you. You think that everything you know is valuable to them but you fail to realize that a lot of what they know is valuable to you."

Dr. Helle goes back to Alaska about every two years and sometimes tours the state, encouraging Alaskan students to consider a career in medicine. The Alaska Native Brotherhood has determined that she is the first Native Alaskan medical-school graduate. Dr. Helle bears this title proudly, saying, "I am the first Native Alaskan to graduate from medical school, and I happen to be a woman."

Dr. Helle suffered a stroke in February 1995 but is now recovering at her home in San Diego. She says the most important advice she has to pass on to the next generation is "just believe in yourself . . . Believe in God and believe in yourself."

Eskimo and female, Loretta Snyder Helle has faced discrimination with a determination to excel. Refusing to be discouraged when 100 percent was required, she took up the challenge and gained a respected place in American society.

GEORGE
BLUE SPRUCE JR.

Pueblo Dentist
(1931–)

Before 1955, the Indian Health Service (IHS) was under the administration of the Bureau of Indian Affairs (BIA). Operating on a limited budget, the BIA had inadequate funds to provide medical care and even less money for dental care. With few dentists in the service, each IHS dentist made rounds to several reservations.

A dentist visited each reservation elementary school two to four times a year. He usually set up his portable "office" in some out of the way place, maybe the basement or a restroom. Children who needed dental care lined the hall and waited in fear. One after another, the young patients were seated in a folding chair that was positioned near a stand that held the dentist's instruments. Teeth were pulled without anesthesia. Those waiting in the hall listened to the cries of the patients being treated.

Dr. George Blue Spruce Jr. remembered waiting in such a line as a child. He wrote in a paper presented to other dentists in 1961: "The memories of such treatment are still clear in the minds of our patients on the reservations today. From such treatment have grown strongly held impressions that dental care means pain and consists of no more than pulling of teeth." Based on his own experience, he has stressed the importance of understanding the Indian's attitude toward dentistry that stemmed from unpleasant past experience.

George Blue Spruce Jr. was born January 16, 1931, in Santa Fe, New Mexico. His father, George Blue Spruce Sr., a cabinetmaker, came from the Laguna Pueblo (village). His mother, Juanita Cruz, a cook at the Santa Fe Indian School, came from the San Juan Pueblo. George is a full-blooded Pueblo Indian and part of the first generation to have parents from different pueblos. The Pueblo derive their name from the early Spanish explorers of the Southwest who called them *Pueblo* (Spanish for town) because they lived in towns or villages. The San Juan Pueblo is located north of Santa Fe and the Laguna Pueblo is located west of Albuquerque, New Mexico.

George's grandmother gave him his Pueblo name, Fon-Ten-Bay-Stehn. The name means "Snow White Bow." George's mother often helped him look for the whitest clouds in the sky and told him his name meant a hunting bow made from those clouds.

Although George grew up near the Santa Fe Indian School where his parents worked, he attended St. Michael's, an all-boys Christian Brothers school in Santa Fe. In the summers he visited his grandparents in the Laguna and San Juan Pueblos.

Young George looked up to his father and was impressed by the perfection and exactness required in cabinetmaking and drafting. George thought about learning drafting and becoming an architect. George Blue Spruce Sr. died when George Jr. was twelve.

During his high school years, George played tennis and participated in youth activities in the community. One of the volunteers in the youth program encouraged George and gave him special attention. Dr. Blue Spruce remembers Doc Renfro as "a take-charge sort of guy . . . friendly to a shy boy who was probably the only Indian participating in the events." George liked Doc and looked up to him. When he heard that Doc was a dentist, George decided he wanted to be a dentist too. With good grades and leadership experience as president of his junior and senior class in high school, George graduated class valedictorian. He also played tennis and won the Santa Fe High School City Championship Tournament in 1949. With all these achievements, he seemed to be a good candidate for dental school; however, the high school guidance counselors discouraged him from seeking a career in dentistry. According to their thinking, he had three strikes against him: one, an Indian had little chance of getting into dental school; two, he probably wouldn't complete the courses; and, three, he couldn't expect to have a successful dental practice in the Santa Fe area.

At that time, about 1950, the Indian Health Service was still a branch of the Bureau of Indian Affairs. Its limited funds provided inadequate staffing for hospitals and clinics. As a result, some clinics were only open part time. In some instances, one dentist serving several reservations was responsible for 20,000 or more people. A dentist with so many patients could provide only emergency care. In other words, he pulled teeth. He practiced no preventative care and no reconstruction, such as fillings and false teeth.

Dr. Blue Spruce wrote in a paper many years later that

> Even as late as 1955 a majority of the American Indians had never had the services of a dentist, and there were many more who had never had any kind of restorative dental treatment. When the Public Health Service's Division of the Indian Health was created and given responsibility for health services for American Indians, dental care became for the first time an integral part of the Indian's health picture, and dentistry became a profession to be proved, elevated, and recognized in its own right.

Although George's experience with the dentist who visited the Santa Fe Indian School left unpleasant memories, he was determined to pursue a career in dentistry. Probably the most important factors contributing to his success were a role model and motivation. Although his counselors told him he couldn't do it, George thought he could—and found a way.

When he told the local Elks Club that he wanted to be a dentist, they gave him their full support. They offered him a scholarship to pay his tuition and help with expenses. George supplemented his scholarship with part-time jobs. He worked as a taxi driver, night watchman, and beef lugger in a meat-packing plant.

He received his doctor of dental surgery degree from Creighton University in Omaha, Nebraska, in 1956. He was the first American Indian dentist in the United States.

After graduation, he served two years in the United States Navy as a lieutenant in the Dental Corps. He was the dentist for the 105-member crew of the *Nautilus*, the first U.S. atomic submarine, prior to its historic cruise beneath the North Polar ice cap. For his service, Dr. Blue Spruce received a citation from the navy.

After he was discharged from the navy in 1958, Dr. Blue Spruce began a distinguished career with the U.S. Public Health Service. By this time the responsibility for Indian health care was transferred from the Bureau of Indian Affairs to the Public Health Service. After this shift, in 1955, dentistry on the reservations improved. For one thing, the Indians who served in World War II knew that better dental care was available. While in the military they learned that teeth could be saved with fillings, and that missing teeth could be replaced with bridges and dentures. Furthermore, military dentists introduced them to anesthetics and less painful dental procedures. When they returned home, Indian veterans wanted to receive dental care on the reservation comparable to that they received while in military service.

As dental care improved on the reservations, the war veterans became willing dental patients. The memory of having teeth pulled without anesthetic lingered in the minds of other tribe members, however, and they continued to shun the dentist's office.

Dr. Blue Spruce wanted Indians to have better dental care that included fillings and tooth replacement. Before this could happen, Indian patients had to be willing to visit the dentist. In order to make them more willing patients, Dr. Blue Spruce saw the need to educate the Indians about the importance of dental care to their health. He also wanted them to experience less painful dentistry from kind, gentle, and more understanding dentists. He thought this would likely change Indians' negative attitudes about dentistry. In a paper he presented at the Public Health Service Clinical Society in Lexington, Kentucky, in April 1961, Dr. Blue Spruce promoted the idea that dentists had to earn the trust of their patients through sincerity and kindness. He said, "Indians can detect with extraordinary accuracy the individual who is sincere . . . A dental officer who, besides exercising his professional ability, shows his genuine desire to work for the total well-being of his Indian patients will see true gratitude in their actions and attitudes." He predicted that the time would come when "the American Indian will equal his non-Indian neighbor in recognizing the importance of complete dental care." That year, Dr. Blue Spruce received the United States Public Health Service Award for the best scientific paper presented at their annual meeting.

After acquiring a master's degree in public health from the University of California at Berkeley in 1967, Dr. Blue Spruce went to South America as consultant in dental health to the World Health Organization of the United Nations. In this capacity, he taught courses throughout South America from 1968 to 1970.

After returning to the United States, Dr. Blue Spruce chalked up an impressive list of high-level positions in the Washington offices of Health, Education and Welfare in programs that deal with Indian health care. During this time, he gained the respect of his colleagues and legislators. This gave him the opportunity to influence legislation that created new programs, such as the Health Manpower Training Act of 1971. This legislation addressed the shortage of health care professionals and provided funds for training and scholarships for students entering this field. The legislation provided special attention to areas of greatest need, which included Indian health care. To implement the act, the Office of Health Manpower Opportunity was created in 1972 and Dr. Blue Spruce was appointed director. In this capacity he worked to encourage more Indian students to consider becoming dentists, physicians, and other health professionals. Dr. Blue

Dr. Blue Spruce, wearing the uniform of the Commissioned Corps of the U.S.
Public Health Service, when he was director of the Phoenix Area IHS.
(Courtesy of George Blue Spruce Jr.)

Spruce left Washington in 1979 to return to the Southwest, where he assumed the position of director at the Phoenix Area Indian Health Service.

As director, Dr. Blue Spruce held the title of assistant surgeon general with a Public Health Service rank of rear admiral. Dr. Blue Spruce is the first American Indian dentist to hold this office. As director of this large IHS area, his responsibilities included administering the health care delivery system for approximately 105,000 Indians in Arizona, Nevada, and Utah. The Phoenix area Indian medical facilities include a large medical center in Phoenix and eight reservation hospitals, in addition to seven health centers and six health stations.

After his retirement from the IHS in 1990, Dr. Blue Spruce took a leading role in organizing the Society of American Indian Dentists and agreed to serve as president of the organization. He continues to hold that position. As a leader among Indian health professionals, Dr. Blue Spruce encourages other professionals to seek leadership roles. In his words, "Indian health practitioners have a special understanding of their communities. It is important for those with professional credentials to work toward leadership roles in which they can help other Indians improve both their education and their health services."

Dr. Blue Spruce has received many awards and honors during his career. He was named the Outstanding American Indian of the Year at the American Indian Exposition at Anadarko, Oklahoma, in 1972. The American Indian Council Fire presented him with the Outstanding American Indian Achievement Award of 1974. Many consider this award the highest honor bestowed by the Indian community. He received the Award of Merit presented by the Association of American Indian Physicians in August 1980. This award recognized his significant contributions toward raising the level of health care of the American Indian and native Alaskan. Creighton University named Dr. Blue Spruce Alumnus of the Year in 1984, in recognition of his distinguished service to his fellow man and his alma mater in keeping with the finest traditions of the university. He also received the Association of American Medical Colleges Annual Award, presented to a health professional for contributing to the health of American Indians. In addition, he was named the Most Outstanding American Indian Health Professional by the American Indian Science and Engineering Society.

An avid tennis player throughout his life, Dr. Blue Spruce was the 1977 National Indian Tennis Champion and the 1987 Arizona Senior Olympics gold medalist. In honor of his athletic achievements, he was inducted into the American Indian Athletic Hall of Fame in May 1996, in Phoenix, Arizona.

After experiencing frightening and painful dentistry in his youth, Dr. Blue Spruce understood the reluctance of his people to seek dental care. He encouraged other dentists to understand their Indian patients' fears and work toward building the dentist-patient relationship. Like many others involved in Indian health care, Dr. Blue Spruce sees the need for more Indian health professionals and vast opportunities in IHS careers. He encourages Indian students to aim high and seek influential positions at the top. Dr. Blue Spruce feels that career choices should not be made lightly. He advises those about to make career decisions to "be serious, leave no room for halfway solutions. Once you make up your mind, pursue your goal. Research possible problems and pitfalls before you begin. Then once you've made a decision . . . stick with it. And you're bound to succeed!"

LOIS FISTER STEELE

Assiniboine Physician
(1939–   )

Lois Steele returned to Poplar, Montana, on the Fort Peck Reservation, after graduating from college in 1961. She spent the next few years teaching at area schools. One evening during this time, Lois, her two daughters, and a friend went to a movie in Wolf Point, a small town 22 miles west of Poplar. As they drove down U.S. Highway 2 on the way home, they came upon a serious automobile accident. Six people were involved in the crash. All were badly injured; two were in critical condition. They were bleeding and broken, dazed and frightened. Lois stayed at the scene of the accident while her friend took the girls and went to Poplar to call for help.

Growing up in a large family in a rural area, Lois had bandaged her siblings' small wounds and sometimes cared for injured animals. She had no formal medical training and no experience in dealing with such overwhelming trauma, however. Drawing on her childhood experience and the knowledge gained in college health and zoology classes, she comforted and soothed the injured and administered first aid as best she could.

In the long, crucial moments before an ambulance arrived, Lois found that it wasn't difficult for her to help the injured. "The blood and all . . . emotionally, I could cope," she said as she later recalled the accident. In fact, she found the excitement and sense of urgency exhilarating. Her success in aiding the accident victims awakened her to her potential. That night she realized, for the first time, that she *could* be a doctor. She had what it took and she *wanted* to be a doctor.

The only daughter of Russell and Winona Simons Fister, Lois Fister was born November 27, 1939, in Washington, D.C. Russell Fister, a Norwegian, worked at the Bureau of Indian Affairs. Lois's American Indian heritage is through her mother, a member of the Assiniboine tribe. The Fisters divorced when Lois was four years old, and Winona and Lois returned to their family on the Fort Peck Reservation in Montana.

By that time, their band of the Assiniboine tribe had been living at Fort Peck about 70 years. In 1873, an Executive Order established the reservation as a home for both the Assiniboine and Sioux tribes. The two tribes divided the reservation soon thereafter. The Sioux live in the southeastern area near Poplar and Brockton and the Assiniboine live in the southwestern area around Wolf Point.

The tribe acquired its name long ago. *Assiniboine* means "those who cook with stones." This comes from the practice of heating rocks directly in a fire and then tossing them into a pot of water to make it boil. Food was then cooked in the boiling water.

Family ties have remained strong among the Assiniboine. Adhering to tribal custom, those on the reservation share whatever they have with their relatives and friends. The Assiniboine social system revolves around giving. In fact, the Assiniboine language has twenty-four words that mean give. Each of these expressions has a slightly different meaning to relate to a variety of situations and relationships. However, these generous people often have little to share.

As Lois grew up, there were few job opportunities on the reservation. Those who wanted an education had to go away to boarding schools, and many sought employment off the reservation after graduation. Before federal funds became available for higher education, few could afford to go to college. Times were hard on the reservation, but for those who had the advantage of an education, the door opened to a new life.

Lois's mother remarried and divorced again, raised six children, and faced most of the difficulties other reservation single parents faced. "Mom worked hard and we were always broke," said Dr. Steele, who added proudly, "but, I have a sister teaching at Cornell University in New York, a brother who is president of our tribal community college in Montana, a sister who runs a boys club in Alabama, a brother who is a social worker and one who has a regular job."

Growing up on the reservation with plenty of open spaces nearby, Lois and her friends played in the snow in winter and swam in the creek in summer. They rode horses over the prairie. Many of her friends had horses and, for a short while, so did Lois. Her grandfather paid $25 for an old and very stubborn horse. "He was on his way to the cannery," she recalled.

Lois loved the outdoors and sports. She did not participate in school sports, however, until she went to an off-reservation boarding school during her last two years of high school. (Montana high schools did not offer girls athletics.)

Lois began earning her own money at an early age. She babysat each day after school and began working as a dishwasher in a pool hall when she was twelve years old. At age fourteen she took a job at the Beacon, a drive-in restaurant, and worked there until she finished high school. By then she had worked her way up to manager of the restaurant.

In her early years, Lois did not realize that the knowledge she gained while playing on the prairie would one day help her relate to her patients. Curious about everything, she learned to observe her surroundings closely. She saw, she heard, she felt, she smelled, and she touched. She says that "kids who live in asphalt jungles don't know things like when the crocus come out."

Lois did not accept anything at face value. This included material things as well as those found in nature. When her family got their first telephone, curiosity overwhelmed her. She wanted to know what was inside and how it worked. She didn't rest until she had taken the phone apart, then discovered she could not put it back together. She also swallowed a coin to see how long it would take to pass through her system.

Even with all her curiosity and desire to learn, teenage Lois was willing to end her education after high school. "I never really thought I was going to college when I was growing up," she said later. College became more attractive, however, when she heard that Dorrance (Curly) Steele had been offered a football scholarship. With her high school sweetheart headed for college, Lois decided to go, too. And, her father was willing to pay her tuition and first-year dorm costs.

In fall 1957, Lois enrolled at Jamestown College in Jamestown, North Dakota, but transferred to Rocky Mountain College in Billings, Montana, her second semester. Lois and Curly were married in summer 1958. She continued her studies at Rocky Mountain College until 1960. Curly went into the army and was stationed at Fort Carson. To be near him, Lois transferred to Colorado College in Colorado Springs, where she received her bachelor of arts degree in June 1961 with a 3.75 grade point average. Lois and Curly studied Indian history and took Indian leadership workshops in the summers of 1960 and 1961. "[The workshops] enabled me to better cope with the world and to draw from the strength of the Indian culture. Many of the workshop participants went on to be the national Indian leaders."

After graduation, Lois returned to Montana, where she became the women's physical education instructor at Rocky Mountain College for the 1961–62 term. The next year, although she was offered another contract, she returned to graduate school in Colorado while Curly, who was now out of the army, finished his degree. Facing financial difficulties and marital problems, the Steeles then returned to Montana, where Lois taught at various schools throughout the state. She taught math (seventh grade through advanced algebra), science, and English. She coached girls basketball, track and field, gymnastics, and the dance/drill team. During her years of teaching, Lois pursued a master's degree in biology, with an emphasis on science teaching, at the University of Montana at Missoula on a National Science Foundation fellowship.

As she neared the completion of her master's degree, Lois began to think about furthering her education. Although she was now a single parent with two daughters to raise (she and Curly divorced in 1968), she began to contemplate a career in medicine. Her experience at the scene of the serious accident helped her make the decision.

After receiving her master's degree in 1969, Lois applied for admission to Wayne State Medical School. She traveled to Detroit, Michigan, for the interview. The interviewer considered the twenty-nine-year-old American Indian a poor risk because women often left medical practice to care for their families. Being divorced with children was another mark against her. To make matters worse, the few thousand dollars she saved wasn't enough to pay for medical school. Her application was rejected because of age, race, parental status, and income.

Surprised and disappointed, but not completely discouraged, Lois accepted a teaching position at Dawson College in Glendive, Montana. At Dawson, Lois taught various classes, including human biology, Indian history, and psychology. She also coached women's basketball, track, and the drill team. During her time at Dawson, from 1970 to 1973, she served as dean of women, director of special services and faculty senate president.

Lois Steele left Dawson College to become director of the Indians Into Medicine (INMED) program at the University of North Dakota in March of 1973. Her background in education and her interest in medicine, as well as her race, made her a natural for the position.

The INMED program was developed to help provide a more permanent medical staff to serve Indians on the reservations. The turnover rate in non-Indian doctors is high, in part because they do not understand the culture or speak the language of reservation patients. In addition, they often leave after a few years to seek higher pay and positions in hospitals with better resources. The INMED program was developed by representatives from the twenty-three tribes in the INMED service area, which included North Dakota, South Dakota, Nebraska, Montana, and Wyoming. The recruitment material, designed to encourage and train Indian students for careers in the medical field, included cartoon characters based on Chippewa Indian beliefs passed on in story form from one generation to another. According to these beliefs, the world began when a woman fell from the sky into an endless body of water. Two swans rescued her and took her to the Great Turtle, master of all the animals. He called a council meeting and asked the other animals to bring earth from far below to make an island for the woman. Many animals tried and failed, dying in the attempt. Finally, Old Lady Toad dove down and brought some earth up to Turtle. After placing the earth on his back, she died from exhaustion. The earth on Turtle's back grew into the world we know today. However, there was no light in the sky. Great Turtle called on the powers of the other animals again. Little Turtle was the only one who could take light to the sky. With the help of the other animals she collected the lightning, formed it into a ball, and took it to the sky where it became the sun. She then formed a smaller ball to be the moon. (Many tribes believe a female turtle, instead of a toad, brought up the first earth.)

The INMED symbol was designed by the program's first director, Dr. Lionel deMontigny, a Chippewa physician. The symbol, a turtle (from the myth) with the serpents and staff (the caduceus, symbol of modern medicine), combines traditional Indian culture with modern medicine.

Once established, and stabilized by Lois, INMED encouraged Indians to seek careers in the medical field and return to the reservations to practice. In this way, the medical needs of reservation Indians could be met by doctors who understood their culture and language. With this in common, these doctors were thought to be more likely to stay on the reservation long-term. This unique program prepared the individual Indian for a career and helped bring medical care to the tribes in the service area.

The INMED program expanded under Lois Steele's direction to include summer courses from junior high school through premed levels, plus scholarships and financial aid to American In-

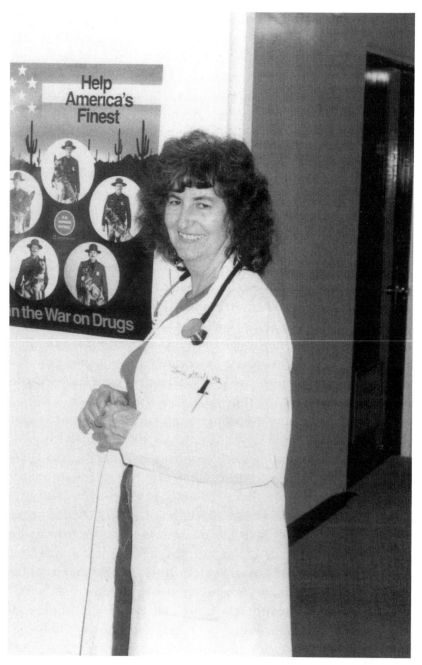

Dr. Lois Steele beside a poster for the War on Drugs. She is involved in most aspects of health care that benefit the Indian population. (Courtesy of Lois Steele)

dian and native Alaskan medical students. The INMED program proved to be so successful that it has served as a model for other minority health career programs.

As director of INMED, Lois personally encouraged Indian students as they worked toward their medical degrees. Dr. Michael T. Vandall, the first medical school graduate under the INMED program, expressed his appreciation for " . . . understanding, encouragement, and moral support from people like Lois Steele . . . "

After working in the INMED program for little more than a year and a half, Lois resigned her position to attend medical school. This time, when she applied, six medical schools welcomed her application. Times had changed and schools now received extra funds for minority students. She chose the University of Minnesota and enrolled in 1974.

Medical school was not easy. In addition to difficult courses and long hours, Lois was older than most other students and was a single parent responsible for two daughters, one in her teens. She took consultant jobs in order to make ends meet. Her finances eased, however, when she received a National Health Service scholarship toward the end of her first year.

Besides financial difficulties, Lois had to overcome prejudice and feelings of insecurity while at medical school. She said, "I had to prove that I was as good as everybody else; some people felt I had gotten in because I am Indian and a woman." In order to prove herself, Lois Steele developed a positive attitude more powerful than her insecurities. Based on her experience she later gave this advice to other students, "Believe in yourself . . . study hard and remember that if you are going to be a good doctor, everything you learn will come in handy at one point or another."

This attitude and hard work paid off for Dr. Steele. She earned the Lampson Award for being the most outstanding woman medical student at the University of Minnesota Medical School at Duluth in 1976. All medical students at Duluth transfer and receive their M.D. degrees from the University of Minnesota at Minneapolis. Lois finished medical school in three and a half years. She was granted her degree in December 1977 and began her internship the following January. She began a family practice residency at Methodist Hospital in St. Louis Park, Minnesota. While working toward completion of her residency, she returned to INMED and resumed her position as director in 1980. This was made possible by special agreement with the dean of the medical school in North Dakota and the head of Indian Health Service.

As director of INMED, Dr. Steele expanded the program budget from $50,000 to more than $1 million. She established an outreach program to Indian schoolchildren on the reservations. The IN-MED Traveling Medicine Show featured puppets and a coloring book to introduce children to possibilities and opportunities in medicine.

While serving as director of INMED, Dr. Steele completed her residency at the University of North Dakota at Grand Forks. She became a board-certified family medicine practitioner in 1984.

Dr. Steele asserts that America has a great need for primary-care providers. She encourages those seeking a career in the medical field to consider becoming family practitioners, nurse practitioners, and physician assistants. She says it is "important to know a little about a lot of things." This includes understanding other cultures. "If you understand the culture of the people you are taking care of, you are halfway there."

Dr. Steele has a respect for traditional healers and encourages other physicians practicing among the Indians to work with them in treating patients. Once, while visiting a reserve village in Canada, she was asked if she was a medicine woman. She replied, "No, I don't know enough. I only know some about Western medicine."

While serving as director of INMED, Dr. Steele practiced medicine in North Dakota, occasionally seeing patients at the Indian Health Service facilities at the White Shield Clinic on the Fort Berthold Reservation and the Fort Yates Indian Hospital on the Standing Rock Reservation.

Dr. Steele left INMED in 1986 and moved from Grand Forks, North Dakota, to Tucson, Arizona, where she took a position in the IHS Research Division. After being sent on a temporary duty assignment to the Pascua Yaqui tribe in the Tucson area, Dr. Steele became clinical director of the Pascua Yaqui Health Department.

As a family practitioner, Dr. Steele's professional interests include all health threats that affect Indians today. She has attended many conferences and presented papers on topics including domestic abuse, AIDS, American Indian women's roles in the feminist movement, cancer prevention and control for American Indians and native Alaskans, American Indians in medical education, stress and hypertension, and substance abuse (especially tobacco abuse).

Dr. Steele has a wide range of interests. "I've tried to study anything that I could . . . just curious," she says. Besides her medical practice and research, Dr. Steele participates in community affairs. She has served as an assistant Cub Scout master, worked in PTA, served on the United Way board, and as deacon in the Holy Way Presbyterian Church in Tucson.

Throughout her career, Dr. Steele has received many prestigious awards, including the Outstanding Educator of America Award in 1970 and the Distinguished Achievement Award from the Rocky Mountain College Alumni Association in 1981. She was named in *Who's Who in North Dakota* in 1984. She received the Indian Health Service Award for Health Promotion Disease Prevention Work and the American Indian Science and Engineering Society Ely Parker Award in 1989. In 1991 she received the Pascua Yaqui Project Head Start Volunteer Award and an IHS award recognizing her for setting up a substance abuse program that includes methadone treatment.

She has a love and compassion for American Indians that reaches beyond her own tribe. With her understanding of the role that culture plays in health care, she has attempted to meet the medical needs of American Indians through research and education. Her work in research satisfies her curious nature. The sharing of her findings reflects the culture of her people, who have always willingly shared whatever they had.

Dr. Steele is best known for her work with INMED. Many Indian physicians in practice today were encouraged by Dr. Steele and found financial backing for their education through her efforts. With a background in education and a ravenous appetite for knowledge, Dr. Steele lives out her personal belief that "anyone can use everything that they learn . . . no matter what it is."

LORI ARVISO
ALVORD

Navajo Surgeon
(1958–   )

The Navajo Indians migrated south from northwestern Canada and Alaska between 1,000 and 600 years ago. They lived the nomadic life of hunters and gatherers before their arrival in the southwestern desert. In order to survive the arid conditions, they observed the Spaniards and Pueblo Indians already settled in the area. From contact with these people, the Navajo dramatically changed their culture. They began cultivating crops for food and raising sheep for meat and wool. They learned weaving from the Pueblo and soon surpassed the skill of these craftsmen who had been weaving for thousands of years. Today the Navajo are famous for their unique rugs.

With a population of more than 219,000, the Navajo are the largest American Indian tribe in the United States today. Inhabitants of a vast expanse of land, a reservation covering almost 25,000 square miles rich in beautiful scenery and valuable minerals, including coal, uranium, gas and oil, the Navajo remain one of the poorest tribes in North America. In 1995, only 40 percent of Navajo reservation homes had adequate plumbing and only 20 percent had telephones. This compares to nationwide rates for rural areas about fifty years ago. Unfortunately, tribal regulations and federal restrictions have prevented progress into the twentieth century.

An effort is being made to improve the reservation´s health care, that has long been provided by the Indian Health Service (IHS). However, there are too few doctors willing to establish permanent practices on the reservation, even fewer, like Lori Arviso Alvord, the first Navajo woman surgeon, who understand Indians' way of life.

Lori was born in Crownpoint, New Mexico, December 8, 1958, the daughter of Robert and Rita Taylor Cupp. According to Lori, her father's family is Navajo and her mother's is a blend of Western European cultures. Her father worked for the Bureau of Indian Affairs as an electrical technician and later as a construction manager.

In the Navajo culture, the family line is inherited through the mother. Since only Lori's father is Navajo, she must claim her heritage through his mother, her paternal grandmother. "I belong to the Tsinajinni, which translates to 'Dark Forest Clan' or 'Bear People.' I take my father's mother's clan," Lori explains.

Lori attended school in Crownpoint, New Mexico. The small town lies a few miles west of the Continental Divide and east of the Navajo reservation in northwestern New Mexico. As a child, Lori loved to read and found that reading gave her an advantage in all her classes. She graduated from Crownpoint High School in 1975, fourth in her class and a member of the National Honor Society. She remembers herself as "a very ordinary little girl who just played on the mesas." However, she had more than ordinary ability and an outstanding role model in her grandmother.

Lori's grandmother, Grace Arviso Cupp, worked her way up from teacher to principal during her forty-year career with the Bureau of Indian Affairs schools on the Navajo reservation. Watching her grandmother, Lori realized at an early age that "A woman could work at a job and make a difference in people's lives." As Lori grew up in a world with virtually no other role models—no Navajo doctors, no Navajo lawyers, no Navajo engineers—Grace Cupp's profession and her impact on the lives of her students left a lasting impression.

When it came time to think about college, a fellow student gave Lori a stack of brochures. The one displaying a "pretty green campus" drew her attention. As the result of filling out that one application, she was accepted at Dartmouth.

More than 200 years old, the Ivy League college located in Hanover, New Hampshire, nestles among green hills and trees. Across the Connecticut River from Vermont, the campus offered Lori quite a contrast to the red mesas of the Southwest where she grew up.

Homesick and new to college life, Lori found a common bond with the other 35 Indian students on campus. Her studies at Dartmouth included a double major in psychology and sociology, modified with Native American studies. She graduated in 1979.

After graduation, Lori returned to New Mexico and found a job as a biomedical research assistant. Disappointed with the low wages, she gave little thought to continuing her education and much less to going to medical school. Fortunately, her boss recognized her potential and encouraged her to further her education.

Remembering her grandmother and the impact she had on people's lives, Lori decided that she wanted to be a doctor. She was accepted at Stanford University in Palo Alto, California, on an IHS scholarship in 1981. The scholarship had a "payback obligation." In other words, after Lori received her M.D., she would owe IHS one year of service for every year of medical school the program funded. In 1985, Lori graduated from Stanford University Medical School, one of the top medical schools in the United States. She completed her general surgery residency there in 1991.

Realizing the benefits of attending an outstanding college, Dr. Alvord recommends that students seek admission at the best college available to them, even if it means going away from home. "The better the institution you attend, the better education you will receive. Don't be afraid to go away from home to get into a better institution."

After receiving her M.D. from Stanford and completing a six-year surgical residency at Stanford University Hospital, Lori returned to New Mexico, where she took a staff position in general surgery at the Gallup Indian Medical Center. The Medical Center is operated by IHS as part of the Gallup Service Unit, which also includes three clinics. The Gallup Service Unit provides medical care to about 40,000 Native Americans in the 1,000-square-mile area around Gallup, New Mexico. Most are Navajo who live in the city of Gallup and the nearby communities of Twin Lakes, Red Rock, Church Rock, and Naschitti.

Soon after moving back to Gallup, Lori met her future husband, Jonathan Alvord, who was completing his training as a Green Beret medical specialist at the Gallup Medical Center. The couple was married in 1994 and established their home in the Gallup area. When Lori took her husband's name, she dropped her maiden name and added her grandmother's maiden name, Arviso, as her middle name to honor her Navajo family. Although Jonathan is not American Indian, the Alvords named their first son Christopher Kodiak. Dr. Alvord chose this name "because we have a strong connection in our family to bears . . . our clan is symbolized by bears." Young Kodi, as he is called, receives his Navajo heritage through his mother's line, the Dark Forest Clan, or Bear People.

After fulfilling her three-year payback obligation, Dr. Alvord continued in her position at the Indian Medical Center. In fact, after five years, she has no plans to leave. The desire to return to her people and help meet their health needs motivated her to go to medical school. "The Indian population deserves to have permanent physicians and, if possible, Indian physicians, people who understand their culture and way of life," she said.

Although few doctors go to the Indian Medical Center to establish a medical practice, Dr. Alvord never thought of going anywhere else. In fact, in order to staff hospitals, doctors often must be lured to the reservation in exchange for repayment of student loans. As a result, many doctors only stay long enough to fulfill National Health Service core requirements to pay back scholarship commitments.

Dr. Alvord sees a tremendous need for the Navajo people to have the opportunity to develop a trust between patient and doctor. She said, "When they trust me, that helps with the overall outcome of the surgery. They need to understand what is going to happen in the course of the treatment and trust the people who are providing their care." Seeing the same doctor each visit, over a period of time, helps establish this trust.

In addition to her surgery schedule, Dr. Alvord makes regular rounds at a small clinic operated by Indian Health Services at the Crownpoint Hospital. Navajo patients overflow the waiting room and line the halls awaiting treatment. Holding to tribal tradition, many Navajo delay modern medical treatment until after they visit a medicine man. When their symptoms persist, they go to the clinic as a last resort. Vulnerable to superstition and frightened of unfamiliar hospital surroundings and high technology, Navajo patients respond better to doctors who understand their culture. Knowing this, Dr. Alvord combines her knowledge of medicine and Navajo beliefs to gain the confidence of her patients.

Dr. Alvord's Navajo heritage, evident in every aspect of her life, contributes to the way she relates to her patients. In the Navajo culture, there is an emphasis on how you relate to everything around you. "We call it *nizhoni*," she says. "It is the Navajo concept of how to live. Basically it is a philosophy with an emphasis on maintaining harmony in your life. All aspects of your life relating to family, tribe, clan, environment, animals . . . all things must be in balance, avoiding excesses." This philosophy forms the core of the Navajo way of life. Even the distinctive Navajo rug designs, themselves masterpieces of harmony and balance, reflect this philosophy.

According to traditional Navajo beliefs, friendly and hostile forces dwell in the universe. All is well as long as these forces are kept in harmonious balance. Disturbance of this harmony may bring about illness, death, or some other disaster. Accordingly, the Navajo believe that supernatural forces cause all illness, mental as well as physical.

Dr. Alvord believes strongly that traditional Navajo practices must be incorporated into modern medicine in order to treat

Navajo patients. In other words, she sees a need to build a bridge between the two worlds by combining ancient rituals and modern technology. She has asked the Gallup Indian Medical Center to bring in a medicine man to perform Navajo healing ceremonies. In addition, she recommends that plans for future hospitals include a room for holding sings, or chantways. Dr. Alvord thinks that a sing may be the best treatment for some illnesses, such as depression. However, she highly recommends surgery for other ailments, such as breast lumps or diseased gallbladders.

Navajo medicine men perform chants (a combination of prayers, myths, and poetry rendered in song) to cure patients by bringing them back in balance and harmony with the forces of the universe. Each Navajo medicine man, or singer, knows at least thirty-five chants. One chant may contain as many as 500 songs.

Along with the words to these songs, each medicine man also knows several designs for sand paintings to be used with the chant. Each chant is designed for a specific illness. For example,

Dr. Lori Alvord, ready for a typical day of rounds at the Crownpoint Hospital. (Michael Heller for NYT pictures)

the Mountain Chant cures nervous disorders. The singer pre-scribes treatment for the individual patient, selecting only certain songs and sand paintings from the chant.

A chantway (a performance of selected songs and sand-paint-ing ceremonies along with purification rites) may last several days. The chantway can be performed according to one of three rituals: the Holyway, which restores health to the "one sung over" by attracting good; the Evilway, which brings healing by exorcis-ing (getting rid of) evil; or the Lifeway, which heals injuries. Sand painting is used during all Holyway ceremonies and most Evil-way ceremonies, but is never used in Lifeway ceremonies.

Before the ceremony begins, the medicine man and his helpers work for hours to create a sand painting. They skillfully trickle crushed sandstone, pollen, cornmeal, crushed flower petals, and charcoal from their fingers. Slowly, a beautifully colored mosaic appears, depicting events in the life of a supernatural being. The patient sits or lays on the sand painting during the curing cere-mony. Power is thought to be absorbed from the sacred objects depicted in the sand painting. During the chant, the patient relives events in the life of an ancient hero who was cured by the Holy People. Each sand painting must be destroyed before sunset and another painted the next day if needed.

Many of the curing chants originate in the Blessingway cere-mony, the backbone of the Navajo religion. This ceremony is used frequently (like preventive medicine) to keep harmony and bal-ance in the lives of those who are "sung over." The Blessingway ceremony promotes the Navajo concept of *nizhoni*.

To Dr. Alvord, performing surgery is a powerful, spiritual experience, a part of the healing process that brings the ailing body back into balance and harmony. "What an amazing and rare thing it is to actually work inside another human being . . . " she said in an interview. "I feel an unbelievable link to something larger—call it God . . . a universal spiritual connectedness."

With her understanding of Navajo culture and tradition, Dr. Alvord can calm fears in her patients other physicians might not recognize. Working with their faith in the supernatural creates an attitude that promotes healing, whereas violating the Navajo way, even unintentionally, can destroy the trust the patient has in the doctor. In her desire to promote better health care for her people, Dr. Alvord is working on a book, tentatively titled *The Silver Bear and the Scalpel*, about her work with the Navajo people and her interest in blending Navajo tradition with modern medicine.

Dr. Alvord says Indian hospitals need more doctors, especially those who intend to stay and build trust with their patients. She encourages students to consider going into the medical field. "Follow your dreams. Perhaps motivation and hard work carry you further than innate intelligence . . . in other words you might not be a genius but sometimes people who are motivated and work harder go further. Believe in yourself because that is what makes things possible."

EVERETT RHOADES

Kiowa Professor of Medicine
(1931–   )

Mount Scott, the highest peak of the Wichita Mountains in southwestern Oklahoma, is known to the Kiowa as Big Mountain. The land surrounding the mountains was once the Kiowa campgrounds and later the site of a reservation shared with the Comanche and a few Apache. These tribes waged a decade-long battle to keep their reservation lands from being alloted to outside settlers. In the end, the tribes lost the struggle. In 1901, the government opened the reservation lands to settlement. Prior to the land lottery for white settlers, each member of the tribe received an allotment of 160 acres. Many chose land where they had already established a home. The number of small farms nestled among the rolling hills increased as the white lottery winners acquired homesteads in Indian Territory in Oklahoma. The increased population attracted merchants, bankers, and builders. Small towns sprang up almost overnight and grew rapidly.

Everett Rhoades, the grandson of both a Connecticut physician and an Oklahoma Kiowa, learned to walk the path of two cultures successfully. He became a prominent physician and professor of medicine at Oklahoma University while participating in tribal government and cultural activities.

Everett Rhoades was born October 24, 1931 in southwestern Oklahoma. Meers, his hometown, is in the heart of the Wichitas, near Mount Scott. His father, Lee Rhoades, was an elementary school teacher and principal. His mother, Dorothy Rowell Rhoades, also taught elementary school in the same rural area of Oklahoma.

Everett, who is considered half Kiowa, derives his Indian heritage from his mother, who is technically "four-quarters Kiowa" but only half Kiowa by blood. This unique situation came about as the result of regulations designed to determine those who should be on Kiowa tribal rolls. According to these regulations, all those who received Kiowa land allotments were considered "four-quarters Kiowa." According to Parker McKenzie, Ph.D., the oldest member of the Kiowa tribe in 1996 and an expert in tribal history and the Kiowa language: "In the early spring of 1901, the KCA [Kiowa-Comanche-Apache] Reservation was dissolved as such and all recognized enrollees [according to the 1900 census processed by the BIA (Bureau of Indian Affairs) at Anadarko, Oklahoma] were allotted 160 acres." Dorothy Rowell, about three years old at the time, received a land allotment and thus the designation four-quarters Kiowa.

Everett's maternal forebears also include a long line of physicians. His maternal great-grandfather and great-uncle were physicians and members of a prominent Connecticut family. His grandfather followed the family tradition, graduating from medical school in 1895. Extremely interested in Indians, he is said to have visited every Indian reservation. He liked the Kiowa-Comanche-Apache Reservation in Oklahoma best. He traveled there by train sometime after he had contracted tuberculosis. Members of the Kiowa tribe met him at Chickasha, Oklahoma, and took him by wagon to their camp near Mount Scott. By this time, his disease had progressed and he was very ill. The Kiowa nursed him back to health. In fact, he recovered from tuberculosis. While staying with the Kiowa, he met and married a Kiowa woman, Mahbonne. Thus, a branch of the prominent Connecticut Rowell family took root in Indian Territory. Their daughter Dorothy married Lee Rhoades and they had a son they named Everett.

Everett Rhoades grew up on his mother's allotted land. A large group of Kiowa lived in the area, including several of his aunts and uncles. He attended a one-room grade school where his father taught. He then went to high school in Elgin, a nearby town located between Fort Sill and Anadarko. Everett loved sports. Since he stopped growing about the time he started high school, he warmed the bench more than he played. However, his height was not an academic drawback. Everett had an intense fascination with learning new things. Moving from the one-room school to the larger high school opened a new world of knowledge to him. As he tackled algebra and other high-school subjects, he found he needed a new set of learning skills. Grade school had been easy, but high school offered him a delightful challenge.

About this same time, another avenue of learning became available to him. After the end of World War II in 1945, the Kiowa experienced a revival of traditional dancing and powwows. The Forty-nine, a purely social dance, became popular. Almost every Saturday night, the Kiowa gathered at someone's farm around Anadarko for a Forty-nine dance. The younger Indians especially enjoyed this social activity.

The end of World War II also brought a revival of two important tribal societies, the Gourd Clan and the Black Legging Society. The Southern Cheyenne originated the Gourd Clan and the Gourd Dance, which replaced the outlawed Sun Dance. The government banned this dance, too, but after World War II, American Indians revived it in honor of those who lost lives and limbs in the war. Many tribes, as well as the Kiowa, attend Gourd Dances held on the Fourth of July each year. But the Black Legging Society (the highest and most elite order of Kiowa warriors in ancient times but now a veterans honor society) remains strictly Kiowa. The

Black Legging Dance, held twice a year on Veterans and Armed Forces Day, honors those who have served in the military.

Everett Rhoades was taken into the Black Legging Society in 1967 and the Gourd Clan in 1970. He described initiation into these organizations this way: "Leaders come and take you by arm and pull you into the dance. You are initiated into the societies during the dance."

Dances have always been an important part of the American Indian culture. In the past, most tribes danced in preparation for, or in celebration of, many events, such as war, a hunt, planting time and harvest. Today, dances are mostly performed during powwows. Some have significant meaning, like the Gourd Dance and Black Legging Dance, while others are purely social and fun.

A powwow might be described as an American Indian convention. Indians come from near and far to join the festivities. They socialize with old friends and make new ones while they reminisce about the old ways and work to preserve their rich heritage. Many join in traditional dancing and singing.

Singing is considered one of the most important parts of the powwow. In fact, without the singers there would be no dance. Originally songs were sung in the native language of the singer. Many of the original words related religious feelings of joy and mourning. Today, however, because so few people speak the original languages, the words of many of the old songs have been changed to vocables. Vocables are groups of letters that represent sounds that anyone can sing. Since high school, Everett has participated in dancing and enjoyed powwows.

Everett graduated from Elgin High School in 1949. When it came time to think about college, he read in his local Oklahoma newspaper that Lafayette College in Easton, Pennsylvania, and the Zeta Psi fraternity were offering a scholarship for a student of Indian descent. He applied and received the scholarship. Later that year, half a continent away from home, Everett missed the dancing and the powwows. Although he was homesick the whole time he attended Lafayette, he continued his studies there three years before applying for medical school at the University of

Oklahoma. He did not graduate from Lafayette, but at that time, a bachelor's degree was not required to enter medical school.

Everett began his medical studies in 1952 at the University of Oklahoma. When he transferred from Lafayette, however, he forfeited his scholarship. Finances became the greatest obstacle to his completing his education. He received a small loan and grant from the BIA, and a John Hay Whitney Opportunity Scholarship. Rhoades married Bernadine Toyebo (a full-blooded Kiowa) during his second year of medical school. Bernadine shouldered some of the financial burden. She worked full time as a secretary while Everett continued his studies. Graduating from medical school in 1956, Dr. Rhoades was the first Kiowa to obtain a medical degree.

Dr. Rhoades and his wife moved to the Panama Canal Zone, where he interned in 1956 and 1957 at Gorgas Hospital. The first of their five children was born in the Canal Zone. The Rhoades then returned to their home state and Everett entered a residency program at the University of Oklahoma in July 1957. He enlisted in the U.S. Air Force as a captain in September of that year and continued his residency at the university. He completed his four-year residency in internal medicine in 1961.

Since the United States Air Force funded his residency, Dr. Rhoades incurred a five-year payback obligation. This he fulfilled at the regional teaching hospital at Lackland Air Base, San Antonio, Texas.

His obligation to the Air Force completed, Dr. Rhoades accepted a position on the faculty of the College of Medicine at University of Oklahoma in 1966. His Kiowa name, Dau-ahlm-gya-toyah, means "One who makes a quest for healing power [knowledge]." Dr. Rhoades has not only made the quest for healing power, but he has helped others in their quest as well. Having once faced the financial difficulties of medical school, Dr. Rhoades has found a way to help ease that burden for the most outstanding Indian student graduating from his high school alma mater. In 1968, he established the Dorothy Rowell Rhoades Prize at Elgin High School in honor of his mother.

Throughout his distinguished career, Dr. Rhoades has been active in the Indian community. Listed on the rolls of the tribe as

Dr. Rhoades in Kiowa Gourd Clan regalia.   (Courtesy Everett Rhoades)

one-half Kiowa, Dr. Rhoades inherited much of his physical appearance from his white ancestors. As a result, he has encountered prejudice because he does not "look Indian." He has won acceptance among the Kiowa, however, and has been elected to the Tribal Council twice. He served as vice chairman of the tribe in the 1980s. As a result of this high office, he spent much of his free time participating in social and economic projects for the tribe. Still a member of the Gourd Clan and Black Legging Society, his camp can always be found at the celebrations of these organizations on the Fourth of July and Veterans Day.

Dr. Rhoades helped found the Association of American Indian Physicians (AAIP) in 1971. Dr. Rhoades served on the AAIP board of directors for several years and as president in 1972 and 1976. The organization's goal is: "to raise the health status of American Indians and Alaska Natives to a level equal to that of the predominant non-Indian population." In order to accomplish this, more Indians are needed in all fields of medicine. In its effort to help meet this need, AAIP attempts to link every American Indian and native Alaskan health professions student with a member of AAIP who will provide guidance, counseling, and encouragement.

Dr. Everett Rhoades became the first Indian to hold the office of director of Indian Health Service in February 1982. This office accords the rank of assistant surgeon general and is a presidential appointment that must be confirmed by Congress. The director of Indian Health Service holds the rank of rear admiral in the Commissioned Corps of the Public Health Service. After confirmation by Congress, the director is officially sworn in and wears a Public Health Service uniform.

The Indian Health Service (IHS) is an agency of the United States Public Health Service in the Department of Health and Human Services. The IHS operates an extensive health services delivery system for approximately 1.3 million American Indians living on reservations and nearby rural communities, many of whom have retained their tribal traditions. The federally recognized Indian tribes and native Alaska corporations have a government-to-government relationship with the United States. This relationship was established in the 1830s by the Supreme Court.

In the first treaty between these governments (with the Winnebago tribe in 1832), the United States government agreed to provide "physician services" as partial payment for rights and property ceded to the United States by the Indians. Additional agreements have been made, including the Snyder Act of 1921, which authorizes Indian health services by the federal government. At first, the Indian Health Service was administered by the Bureau of Indian Affairs. Later, in 1955, it came under the Department of Health and Human Services as part of the Public Health Service.

Dr. Rhoades is proud of what he has accomplished as director of IHS. The number of IHS physicians and nurses has almost doubled; all IHS hospitals except one were accredited (met estab-

Dr. Everett Rhoades   (Courtesy Everett Rhoades)

lished hospital standards); the IHS budget increased by more than $1 billion; Indian mortality (death) rates were reduced significantly; and the number of outpatient clinic visits increased substantially. During this time, IHS established a cancer detection and prevention program, a chronic diseases center, and links to organizations, including the American Cancer Society, National Cancer Institute, Centers for Disease Control, and the American Red Cross. All of these accomplishments have brought better health care to American Indians.

After serving as director of IHS for nine years, Dr. Rhoades retired from the service in 1993 and returned to the University of Oklahoma. He now holds two positions at the University of Oklahoma: associate dean for community affairs in the College of Medicine and adjunct professor of medicine. His major duty as dean is to encourage interest in enrollment in medical school among Indian students and to support Indian students already enrolled in medical school at the University of Oklahoma. Dr. Rhoades is also associated with Johns Hopkins University's School of Public Health as director of education initiatives for the Center for American Indian and Alaskan Native Health. Dr. Rhoades is also adjunct professor of International Public Health at Johns Hopkins. In this capacity, he supervises a course for graduate students entitled Native American Health. He also conducts short training sessions to help health professionals plan local health programs.

Dr. Rhoades has received many awards during his career. These include the AAIP Outstanding Achievement Award, in 1975, and the Award of Excellence, in 1980. He received the Public Health Service Commendation Medal in 1982, the Meritorious Service Medal in 1985, and the Surgeon General's Medallion (highest award) "for a decade of exemplary leadership of the Indian Health Service and for the development of programs to improve the health of American Indians and Alaska Natives," in 1992.

In 1988, the Kiowa tribe recognized Dr. Rhoades for his service. The citation read, for "exemplary contributions to [the] health of Native Americans . . . while maintaining the cultures and traditions which Native Americans hold in high esteem. This award represents the love Kiowa people have for you, and for the honor bestowed upon them through your achievements."

In 1995, the University of Oklahoma College of Medicine honored Dr. Rhoades with the establishment of the Everett R. Rhoades Prize to recognize outstanding American Indian graduates.

Dr. Rhoades sees enormous opportunity in the health care field. He said, "I don't know of many professions that let a person do so many things. You can teach, be a physician, nurse, pharmacist, physical therapist, X-ray technician, lab technician, receptionist, administrator, or accountant. Health care has to be one of the most rewarding things a person can do."

Dr. Rhoades agrees with many others who think that American Indians are well-suited for the health care field. He encourages Indian students to seek medical careers and never assume that they cannot succeed. He advises students who want to prepare themselves for medical school to "develop such a love of study that they thoroughly enjoy learning."

With a love for learning and a love of his people, Dr. Rhoades is, in the words of Carlos Montezuma, "A man among men." He has successfully walked the paths of two cultures. A former director of Indian Health Services, a physician, and professor at two of the most respected universities in America, Dr. Rhoades has also kept strong ties to his family and tribe. Although he lives in Oklahoma City, he makes regular trips to attend church services at the Mount Scott Methodist Mission where he grew up. He says his family has bridged the cultures "professionally, religiously, and socially." When he retires, Dr. Rhoades plans to return to his people full time and become more involved in the Kiowa community near Meers, Oklahoma.

SELECTED BIBLIOGRAPHY AND FURTHER READING LIST

Introduction

Bowers, Alfred. *Mandan Social and Ceremonial Organization*. Chicago: University of Chicago Press, 1950. In 1930 Alfred Bowers lived among the Mandan for six months. During this time he studied their culture and interviewed the elders of the tribe in an attempt to record and preserve their culture. This book resulted from that study and recounts many aspects of tribal life as remembered by the elders. Bowers is considered an authority on the Mandan people.

"Herbal Healing Is Growing," *WebNews*, December 3, 1995. A feature story posted on the Internet that contains numerous quotes from experts on herbal medicines, including Professor Norman Farnsworth of the University of Illinois at Chicago and Varro E. Tyler of Purdue University.

McKenzie, Parker. Correspondence with the author. Dr. McKenzie, an expert on Kiowa language and the oldest member of the Kiowa tribe in 1996, is extremely knowledgeable about tribal history. Through correspondence, he generously shared his vast research and knowledge of Kiowa history and culture with the author.

Nye, W(ilbur) S(turtevant). "Medicine Men—A Story of Weird Indian Rites," *The Daily Oklahoman*, November 15, 1936. A lengthy newspaper feature story about medicine men written by Nye while he served in the army at Fort Sill, Oklahoma.

Ta-boodle

Boyd, Maurice. *Kiowa Voices. Vol. I & II*. Fort Worth, Tex.: Texas Christian University Press, 1983. Collections of myths, legends, and folktales along with recollections and explanations of ceremonies and customs told by Kiowa people in an effort to truthfully preserve their heritage.

McKenzie, Parker. Letters to author. Dr. McKenzie is the oldest living member of the Kiowa tribe in 1996. He received a doctor of humane letters, *honoris causa*, from the University of Colorado in 1991. "Citizen-scholar, tribal elder, historian, and respected authority on the language of the Kiowa, Parker McKenzie has contributed vastly to the knowledge and understanding of these ancient people native to Colorado and the Great Plains," stated the university. Dr. McKenzie, a great-grandnephew of Ta-boodle, traces his ancestry through the writings of Lewis and Clark.

Mooney, James. *Calendar History of the Kiowa Indians*. Washington, D.C.: Smithsonian Institution Press, 1979. (reprint from 1895–96)

Nye, Wilbur Sturtevant. Bad Medicine & Good. Norman, Okla.: University of Oklahoma Press, 1962. A collection of stories covering Kiowa history from the 1700s through the 1930s. The stories come from Kiowa who actually took part in the events or recalled them from the accounts of their elders. Accounts of Ta-boodle's surgical skills are found in this book.

— — —. "Medicine Men—A Story of Weird Indian Rites," *The Daily Oklahoman*, November 15, 1936. A lengthy newspaper feature story about medicine men, including an account of Tay-bodal's (Ta-boodle) battlefield surgery, written by Nye while serving in the army at Fort Sill.

The Seventeenth Annual Report of the Bureau of American Ethnology 1895–96. An in-depth study of the Kiowa Indians done by the Department of Anthropology of the Smithsonian Institution.

Coyote Woman, Stays Yellow, and Mrs. Good Bear

Bowers, Alfred. *Mandan Social and Ceremonial Organization*. Chicago: University of Chicago Press, 1950. In 1930, Alfred Bowers lived with the Mandan for six months. During this time he studied their culture and interviewed the elders of the tribe in an attempt to record and preserve their heritage. This book resulted from that study and covers the culture and many accounts of tribal life as remembered by the elders. Bowers is considered an authority on the Mandan people.

Leitch, Barbara A. *A Concise Dictionary of Indian Tribes of North America*. Algonac, Mich.: Reference Publications, Inc., 1979. An easy-to-read reference book containing sketches of Indian tribes, including location, customs, culture, and brief history.

Niethammer, Carolyn. *Daughters of the Earth*. New York: Collier Books, 1977. *Daughters of the Earth* focuses on American Indian women, their place in tribal culture, and lifestyle. Ms. Niethammer includes an account of Stays Yellow based on Alfred Bower's book.

Swimmer

Mooney, James. "Myths of the Cherokee." *Nineteenth Annual Report of the Bureau of American Ethnology*. Washington, D.C.: Government Printing Office, 1900. James Mooney lived among the Cherokee and studied their culture for the Smithsonian Institution in 1887. He listened to the elders and recorded their history, including their beliefs and myths. His findings were published in this lengthy report to the Bureau of Ethnology.

———. "Sacred Formulas of the Cherokee." *Seventh Annual Report of the Bureau of American Ethnology*, Washington, D.C.: Government Printing Office, 1891. Only a portion of the sacred formulas are recorded in this report to the Bureau of American Ethnology. Mooney acquired the notebooks of Swimmer and several other Cherokee medicine men along with oral explanations of formulas. This report probably contains more detailed information about Indian healing than any other source. No other tribe had a written language.

———.*The Swimmer Manuscript*. Washington, D.C.: Government Printing Office, 1932. Mooney did not live long enough to complete his work with the Cherokee formulas. The complete Swimmer manuscript was completed and edited by Frans M. Olbrechts and published in 1932. This book contains an updated overview of the Cherokee culture with an emphasis on medicine men and Swimmer's formulas, written in Cherokee with an English explanation.

Carlos Montezuma

Edmunds, R. David, ed., *Studies in Diversity—American Indian Leaders*. Lincoln, Nebr.: University of Nebraska Press, 1980. A collection of short biographical sketches of American Indian leaders representing several tribes and occupations. This book includes a chapter on Carlos Montezuma written by Peter Iverson.

Iverson, Peter. *Carlos Montezuma and the Changing World of American Indians*. Albuquerque: University of New Mexico Press, 1982. An adult biography of Carlos Montezuma covering his life and career.This book includes several pictures and numerous quotes from Montezuma's writings.

Montezuma, Carlos. *Carlos Montezuma's Papers*, San Diego State University, San Diego, Calif. An extensive collection of Carlos Montezuma's letters and writings. Microfilm.

Ruth Hills Wadsworth

Betzinez, Jason. *I Fought With Geronimo*. New York: Bonanza Books, 1959. The autobiography of an Apache Indian who rode with Geronimo as a young man and lived through lifestyle changes that spanned almost 100 years.

Delano, Jane A., R.N., "The Red Cross," *The American Journal of Nursing*, October 1918. A monthly article in the journal discussing and updating activities of the Red Cross.

Dock, Lavina L., R.N., *A History of Nursing*. New York: G.P. Putnam's Sons, 1912. A non-technical history of nursing focused on the time period between 1882–1912. The text is moderately easy to read and the book includes pictures.

"Hotel Dieu and the School of Nursing." *Password*, Fall 1969. A brief article in the El Paso County Historical Society's quarterly publication that gives a thumbnail sketch of the nursing school at the time Ruth Hills would have attended.

"Rescuing the Child Refugees of France." *The Literary Digest*, September 21, 1918. An article covering the work of the Red Cross with orphaned children in France during World War I.

Chief Two Moon Meridas

"Chief Two Moon Leader of Sioux." *Waterbury Evening Democrat*, Thursday, October 20, 1932. Written two years after the event, this article gives an account of the Oglala Sioux making Chief Two Moon Meridas a chief of their tribe. It includes the wording of the proclamation posted in Waterbury.

Fillius, Thomas J. Interviews with author. Various dates, including March 11, 1996. Mr. Fillius's wife, Loretta R. Nugent, is related to Helen Gertrude Nugent, and the couple has collected extensive memorabilia and research on Chief Two Moon.

Fillius,Thomas J, Loretta R. Nugent, Virginia Tyler, and Varro E. Tyler. "Chief Two Moon Meridas: Indian 'Miracle Man'?" *Pharmacy in History*, January 1, 1995. This article is a brief biography of Chief Two Moon that includes testimonials about his herbal medicines, the contents of his patent medicines, and an overview of his life. He was praised by some while others tried to discredit him.

"Herbal Healing Is Growing." *WebNews*, December 3, 1995. A feature story posted on the Internet about herbal medicines, including the attitude of American medical professionals and quotes from herbal medicine experts, including Professor Norman R. Farnsworth of the University of Illinois at Chicago and Professor Varro E. Tyler at Purdue.

Juliano, Frank. "Chief Two Moon—Quack Medicine Man or True Man of Medicine?" *Waterbury Republican*, October 1, 1989. A report on a lecture by Dorothy Cantor, curator for the Mattatuck Museum in Waterbury, Conn., about her research on Chief Two Moon.

Steinberger, Barbara. "Chief Two Moon: Museum Tells Story of Local Popular Indian." *Waterbury Republican*, October 22, 1983. A newspaper account of Ms. Cantor's lecture, which also includes quotes from people who knew Two Moon and returned to Waterbury for the occasion.

Herbert Burwell Fowler

Dockstader, Frederick J. *Great North American Indians*. New York: Van Nostand Reinhold Company, 1977. A collection of brief biographies of notable American Indians that includes Dr. Eastman and Dr. Fowler.

"Dr. Herbert G. (B.) Fowler, Genetic Psychiatrist, 58: Won Lenin Science Prize," *The New York Times*, January 4, 1977. Dr. Fowler's obituary in *The New York Times* provides an overview of his life and accomplishments.

"Genetics Pioneer Dies in Portland." *The Oregonian*, January 3, 1977. Dr. Fowler's obituary in his hometown paper, which includes the details of his death and an overview of his accomplishments.

Hindley, Meredith. *Braided Lives*. Washington D.C.: Superintendent of Documents, 1995. An anthology of poems and short stories by more than forty authors of diverse cultural backgrounds.

Lamarine, R. "Dilemma of Native Americans´ Health." *Health Education*, 1990. An article covering the alcohol problem among Indians and the cultural reasons contributing to it.

McKosato, Harlan. "Healing Generation Rises to Meet Today's Challenges." *Indian Country Today*, February 16, 1995. A report of the February 9, 1995, meeting between American Indian youth and the Senate Indian Affairs Committee, during which young Indians testified and addressed the challenges they face in today's society. The article quotes youths who testified, as well as committee members.

Sullivan, Ann. "Soviets Honor Portland Psychiatrist with Lenin Prize in Science." *The Oregonian*, November 5, 1976. A newspaper account of Dr. Fowler's winning the Lenin Prize. The article gives a brief summary of his accomplishments and provides details concerning the Lenin Prize.

Loretta Snyder Helle

Beiswenger, James N., ed. *American Indian Doctors Today*. vol. 1. Grand Forks, N. Dak.: University of North Dakota Press, 1976. This is a collection of twenty brief biographies of American Indian health professionals compiled by the Indians Into Medicine (IN-MED) program. Each biography includes the subject's tribal background, education, and professional accomplishments.

Davis, Mary. B. ed. *Native America in the Twentieth Century*. 1994. An encyclopedia of various tribes, including the Inupiat. It includes a brief sketch of the tribe's history and customs and its people today.

Handbook of North American Indians. Washington, D. C.: Smithsonian Institution, 1984. Contains an extensive overview of Eskimo culture and history, with a few black-and-white photographs scattered throughout the chapter.

Helle, Loretta Snyder. Interview with author. January, 1996.

George Blue Spruce Jr.

Beiswenger, James N., ed. *American Indian Doctors Today*. vol. 1. Grand Forks, N. Dak.: University of North Dakota Press, 1976. This is a collection of 20 brief biographies of Indian health professionals compiled by the Indians Into Medicine (INMED) program. Each biography includes the subject's background, education, and professional accomplishments in the medical field.

Blue Spruce, George. Interview with author. March 8, 1996.

Blue Spruce, George, Jr. "American Indians as Dental Patients." *Public Health Reports*, December 1961. In this article, based on a paper presented at the meeting of the Public Health Service Clinical Society in Lexington, Ky., April 5–8, 1961, Dr. Blue Spruce addresses the concerns and fears of Indian patients and suggests ways to overcome their fears. He also speaks of his experience with the visiting school dentist as a child.

Books, Kathy Jo. "Dr. George Blue Spruce—An Indian Voice in the U.S. Public Health Service," *Winds of Change*, September 1986. An overview of Dr. Blue Spruce's IHS career and his philosophy concerning the need for more Indian role models and more Indian professionals in top positions at IHS.

Klein, Barry T. *Reference Encyclopedia of the American Indian*, 7th edition. West Nyack, N.Y.: Todd Publications, 1995. A collection of biographies of notable American Indians. Each biography consists mostly of informational lists of events, accomplishments, and awards received.

Internet sources

"Indian Health Service Fact Sheet," Indian Health Service Home Page.

Lois Fister Steele

Bataille, Gretchen M. *Native American Women, a Biographical Diction-ary.* New York: Garland, 1993. A collection of brief biographical sketches of American Indian women, including Lois Steele.

Beiswenger, James N., ed. *American Indian Doctors Today.* vol. 2. Grand Forks, N.Dak.: University of North Dakota Press, 1982. Brief biographies published by the University of North Dakota, including Indian physicians in various medical fields.

Indian Reservations. Jefferson, N.C.: The Confederation of American Indians, 1986. An overview of Indian reservations, including Fort Peck, detailing land status, history, culture, government, population, tribal economy, climate, transportation, utilities, and recreation.

Klein, Barry T. *Reference Encyclopedia of the American Indian,* 7th edi-tion. West Nyack, N.Y.: Todd Publications, 1995. A collection of biographies of notable American Indians. Each biography consists mostly of informational lists of events, accomplishments, and awards received.

Steele, Dr. Lois. Interview with author. October 1995. In telephone conversations with the author, Dr. Steele talked about her child-hood, college days, teaching career, medical career, and INMED.

Steele, Lois. *Medicine Women.* Grand Forks, N. Dak.: University of North Dakota, 1985. An overview of Indian women in medicine, which includes an American Indian myth, profiles of Indian women in health care careers, personal experiences of Dr. Steele, and information about INMED.

Waldman, Carl. *Encyclopedia of Native American Tribes.* New York: Facts On File, 1988. An alphabetical encyclopedia that briefly covers the history, culture, and present status of more than 150 American Indian tribes, including the Assiniboine.

Wolfson, Evelyn. *From Abenaki to Zuni: A Dictionary of Native American Tribes.* New York: Walker and Company, Inc., 1988. An alphabetical listing of sixty-eight North American Indian tribes describing their customs and lifestyle. The book is easy to read and includes drawings and maps.

Lori Arviso Alvord

Alvord, Dr. Lori Arviso. Telephone interview with author. November 14, 1995.

Cohen, Elizabeth "Navajo, Surgeon, Pioneer." *New York Times*, February 17, 1994. A feature story about Dr. Cupp [Alvord] and her practice at the Indian Clinic in Gallup, which includes details of her education and outlook on life.

National Geographic Society, *The World of the American Indian.* Washington, D.C.: The National Geographic Society, 1974. This book, filled with beautiful color and black-and-white photographs, highlights Indian culture and history and includes information about Navajo sand painting.

Winton, Ben. "Vast Navajo Reservation Still Lacks Basic Services." *The Phoenix Gazette*, May 4, 1995. A newspaper feature story on current conditions on the Navajo reservation; includes statistics.

Internet Sources

The Indian Health Service Home Page on the Internet. A collection of sources and statistics concerning Indian Health Service medical centers and clinics.

The Navajo Home Page on the Internet. An ever-changing collection of information on Navajo culture and tribal concerns.

Everett Rhodes

Beiswenger, James N., ed. *American Indian Doctors Today.* vol. 2. Grand Forks, N.Dak.: University of North Dakota Press, 1982. This is a collection of forty-four brief biographies of Indian health professionals compiled by the Indians Into Medicine (INMED) program. Each biography discusses the subject's background, education, and professional accomplishments in the medical field. This volume contains an updated biography of Everett Rhoades.

— — —.*American Indian Doctors Today.* vol. 1. Grand Forks, N.Dak.: University of North Dakota Press, 1976. This is a collection of 20 brief biographies of Indian health professionals compiled by IN-MED. The subjects' background, education, and professional accomplishments in the medical field are provided. Volume 1 contains a biography of Everett Rhoades.

Rhoades, Dr. Everett. Interview with author. February 1996. Dr. Rhoades discussed his career, outlook on life and plans for the future.

Songe, Gabrielle. "American Indian Warriors Pay Tribute to Veterans." *Tri-State Defender*, November 23, 1994. An article about the Second Annual Heritage Day Program, which contains information about the Black Legging Society and Gourd Dance.

Internet Sources

Indian Health Service Fact Sheet, IHS Home Page, Native American Indians—Powwow Information, PRIDE Home Page Updated February 7, 1996.

Index

Boldface type indicates main readings. *Italic* type indicates illustrations.

A

Adelphics 36
A History of Nursing 48
Ah-tah-zone-mah (Ah-tah)
   and Buffalo medicine 6
Alaska 69, 70, 76, 97
Alberta, Canada 62
alcohol consumption 60, 61–62,
   63–65
alcohol content 52
aloe plant 54
alphabet (Cherokee) xiii, 24
   and medicinal record-keeping
   30
Alvord, Dr. Lori Arviso **97–105**,
   102
   birth 98
   college education 99
   early career 100
Alvord, Jonathan (husband of Lori
   Arviso Alvord) 100
American Institute of the History
   of Pharmacy 60
Apache tribe 45, 105
Arizona 45
Arizona territory 35
aspirin xiii
Assiniboine tribe 14, 87
Atlantic City 57
A-tong-ty (wife of Ta-boodle) 9
Ayunini. *See* Swimmer

B

Bad Medicine & Good 7
ball play ritual 25–27
beads, ritual 25
Bear People (Tsinajinni) 98
bear spirit xi, 14
Bergamo, Raymond 60
Big Arrow 9
   Ta-boodle's surgery on 9–11
Bitter Oil—the Wonder Tonic 54,
   56
Blackfoot tribe 52
Black Legging Society 107–108
black root, for healing 16
bleeding treatment 6
Blessingway 103
blistering treatment 6
Blue Spruce, George, Jr . **78–85**, *83*
   birth 79
   career 81–85
   education 80–81
   honors 84
Bowers, Alfred xiii
Braren, J. S. (pastor) 55
Buffalo Medicine Men 6, 8, 9
buffalo spirit xii, 5–6
bundle. *See* Medicine bag
Bureau of Ethnology 30
Bureau of Indian Affairs 2, 40, 62,
   71. *See also* Indian Health Service
   dental service 78

and Dr. Carlos Montezuma 41–43
and Indian Health Service 80, 112

C

Calendar History of the Kiowa Indians 2
Calomel purge 16
Campbell, Senator Ben Nighthorse 65
Canada 97
Canadian Sisters of Charity 47
Carlisle Indian School 37, 39, 48
Carolina 23
Cavalry, United States 46
ceremony. *See* ritual
Cherokee tribe
   and Confederate army 27
   round-up 24
   white influence 23
Cheyenne Massacre 4–5
Cheyenne tribe 107
Chicago 34
Chief Two Moon Herb Company 54–57, *56*
childbirth 17–21
Chiricahua tribe (Apache) 45
cholera epidemic 5
Civil War 27
Cocuyevah (father of Montezuma) 35
Colorado 3
Comanche tribe 4
Confederate army
   and Cherokee recruits 27
Congress 42
Connecticut 54, 57
Courtney, James 57–58
Coyotero tribe (Apache) 45
Coyote Woman **13-15**, 21
creation myth 27–28
Crow, William Spotted 57
Crow Creek Reservation 62

Cruz, Juanita
   (mother of George Blue Spruce, Jr.) 79
culture 14
   Navajo 101
culture and medicine xi, 65–66, 94, 101
Cupp, Grave Arviso (grandmother of Lori Arviso Alvord) 98
Cupp, Robert and Rita (parents of Lori Arviso Alvord) 98
Custer's Last Stand 13–14
Cut Throat Massacre 3–4

D

Dakota Territory 37
dancing 107
Dartmouth College 99
Delano, Jane. A., R.N. 48
deMontigny, Dr. Lionel 91
dental care 78–79, 80, 82
Dickens family (cousins of Montezuma) 40
diet xi
Dinero (father of Ruth Hills Wadsworth) 45
Dinero, Poco (Pinero, brother of Ruth Hills Wadsworth) 45
discrimination 71–73
Dock, Lavinia L., R.N. 48
Doyem-k'hee 5
Driven, Betty Wind 48
drugs, prescription xiii

E

Eastern Cherokee. *see* Cherokee
Eastman, Charles (grandfather of Herbert Burwell Fowler) 62
Evilway 103

F

faith
   in healing ritual xii, 15, 28
Farnsworth, Professor Norman R. 59

fasting 15
Fister, Russell (father of Lois Fister Steele) 87
Fister, Winona Simons (mother of Lois Fister Steele) 86
flu epidemic 54
formulas, written 30
Fort Duchesne 66
Fort Elliot 4
Fort McDowell 40
Fort Peck Reservation 87
Forty-nine dance 107
Fo-Ten-Bay-Stehn (George Blue Spruce, Jr.) 79
Fowler, Dr. Herbert Burwell **61-68,** *64*
    birth 61–62
    career 66–67
    death 67
    education 63
France, Red Cross nurses in 49
future, attitude toward 65

G

General Allotment Act of 1887 39
gentian plant 54
Gentile, Carlos (purchaser of Montezuma) 35
Georgia 23
Geronimo 46
Glancy, Diane 65
"going to the water" ceremony 25
Good Bear (Mrs.) 13, 14, *19*, **21**
    death 21
    as midwife 21
Gourd Clan 107
gravel root (plant) 32
Green-Corn Dance
    in Cherokee tribe 25

H

Harrison Narcotic Act 52
Health Manpower Training Act (1971) 82

Helle, Dr. Loretta Snyder **69–77,** *74*
    birth 70
    career 75–76
    education 71–73
    illness 73, 77
    internship 74–75
    loss of infant 75
Helle, James (husband of Loretta Snyder) 73
herbal medicine xi, 56–57, 59
Hetherington, James A. 54
Hidatsa tribe 14
Hindle Drug Stores 54
Holyway 103
Hotel Dieu School of Nursing *46,* 47

I

illusion. *See* sleight-of-hand
Indian Citizenship Act 43, 44
Indian Health Service 78, 98
    role 80, 111–113
Indians Into Medicine (INMED) program 90–93
infant care, in Mandan tribe 20–21
Ingalls, George (caretaker of Montezuma) 36
INMED. *See* Indians Into Medicine
International Council of Nurses 48
Inuit tribe 70
Inupiat Eskimos 69
Inupiat tribe 70
iron ore 20
Iron Top Mountain 35

J

Jicarilla tribe (Apache) 45

K

Kansas 3, 7–8
Keller, Maria (wife of Montezuma) 41
Kiowa–Comanche–Apache Reservation 106

Kiowa language xiv, 2–3
Kiowa tribe 3, 105, 107
    and Dr. Everett Rhoades 114
    migration 2

L

Lafayette College 108–109
land allotments 105, 106
land treaty, Cherokee 24
language
    first written xiii
    Kiowa 2
Lawrence Daily Journal 42
Lenin Prize in Science 67
Lewis and Clark 2
Lifeway 103
Like-a-Fishhook 14
Literary Digest 49

M

Mahbonne (grandmother of Dr.
    Everett Rhoades) 107
Mandan Social and Ceremonial Or-
    ganization 14
Mandan tribe 14
Maunte-pah-hodal
    Ta-boodle's surgery on 8–9
McKenzie, Parker, Ph. D. xiv, 2,
    106
Mdewakanton tribe 62
medicine. *See also* herbal medicine;
    plants; power; ritual; white medi-
    cine
    Indian practice xi–xii
    Mandan practice 13
    patent 51
medicine bag xi–xii, 13, 21
medicine men 5
medicine song 15, 16, 28–29,
    102–103
medicine women 21
menstruation 18
mental illness 63, 66

Meridan. *See* Meridas, Chief Two
    Moon
Meridan, Chief Colon (father of
    Chief Two Moon Meridas) 52
Meridas, Chief Two Moon **51-60**,
    53
    birth 52
    death 60
    herbal medicine company 52
    lawsuit against 60
    marriage 52
    philanthropy 57-58
    Rome visit 59
Meridas, Helen Nugent (wife of
    Chief Two Moon Meridas) 60
Mescalero Apache tribe 45
mescal plant 45
Metal Head 7–8
Methodist Church 69
Mexico 45
Michigan 90
Michigan State Medical School 66
midwifery
    in Mandan tribe 17–21
Miles, General 46
Mimbreno tribe (Apache) 45
mineral oil 54
Minnesota 62
missionary presence 69
Missouri River 2
Mogollon tribe (Apache) 45
Mohave Apache 35
Montana 62, 86, 88
Montezuma, Dr. Carlos **34-43**, *38*
    birth 36
    career 37–40
    death 42–43
    education 36–37
    purchase of 35–36
Mooney, James xiii, 27, 32
mortality rate 63
music. *See* medicine song
myth. *See also* power; ritual
    animal 27–28

Chippewa 91
and disease treatment 30–31
plant 28

N

naming practices 2–3
narcotics 51–52
nature
Indian love for xi
Navajo tribe 97
Nevada 39
New Mexico 45, 98
nizhoni 101, 103
North Carolina 27
North Dakota 12, 89
Nugent, Helen Gertrude (wife of Chief Two Moon Meridas) 54
Numakiki (Mandan tribe) 12
nursing profession
Indian women in 47–48

O

Oceti Sakowin 62
ocher, red 20
Odle-pah-yodle (mother of Ta-boodle) 2
Oglala Sioux tribe 58
Ohiyesa 67
Oklahoma 3, 4, 105–106, 113
Oregon 66
Osage 4
owl spirit xii, 5

P

Panama Canal Zone 109
patent legislation 51
payment 18, 31
Peace Corps 75–76
Peah-bo
father of Parker McKenzie 2
periwinkle plant, Madagascan 59
Pharmacopeia of the United States of America xiii
Pima tribe 35

Pinaleno tribe (Apache) 45
Pine Ridge Reservation 58, 62
Pinero 49
Pinero (Poco Dinero, brother of Ruth Hills Wadsworth) 45
pioneer women
and childbirth 20–21
pipe payment 18
plants
medicinal xii–xiii, 28, 54
plaster treatment 6
Platte River 2
Pope Pius XI 59
power, healing 55, 103, 104
transmission xi–xii
powwow 107
property, attitude toward 65
psychiatry, genetic 63
Pueblo tribe 52, 79, 97
Purdue University School of Pharmacy 57
Pure Food and Drug Act 52
purging treatment 6
purification ritual 5

Q

Qualla reservation 27
Queen of the Meadow (plant) 32

R

Rainy Mountain Creek 4
rattlesnake bites 11
Red Cross nurses 44, 48–49
red sage 16
religion xii, 32
remedies, Indian 51–52
reservation life 46–47. *See also* culture
Rhoades, Dr. Everett **105-114**, *110, 112*
birth 106
career 109–111
early education 107
honors 113

ritual 5, 17, 25–27
ritual and medicine xi, xiii,
    101–102, 103
    Apache 47
    purification 25
root. *See also* black root
    medicinal use 14–15
Rowell, Dorothy(mother of Ev-
    erett Rhoades) 106

S

Saddle Mountain Intertribal Burial
    Ground (Kiowa Baptist Church)
    11
sage, for healing 16
sand painting 103
Santee Sioux tribe 62
Sante Fe Indian School 80–81
Saskatchewan, Canada 62
scurvy xi
secretiveness 29–30
Sequoya xiii, 24
shaman. *See* medicine men
singing 107. *See also* medicine song
Sioux tribe 87
Siseton tribe 62
Sixty-ninth Regiment 27
Skenandore, Zippa 48
sleight-of-hand xii, 55
    healing use 15
smallpox epidemic 5, 61
    in Mandan tribe 14
Smithsonian Institution xiii, 13
Smokey Hill River 7–8
smoking xi
snake medicine 17–18
snake vision 17
Snyder, Anna Nelson (mother of
    Loretta Snyder) 70
Snyder Act 112
Society of American Indian Den-
    tists 84
Society of American Indians 41, 42
song. *See* medicine song; singing

South Dakota 58, 62
Soviet Union 67
Stays Yellow 13, **15–21**
    death 21
    as midwife 17–20
Steele, Dorrance (Curly, husband
    of Lois Fister Steele) 89
Steele, Dr. Lois Fister **86–96**, *92*
    birth 87
    college years 89
    early career 90
    early years 88
    family practitioner 94–95
    honors 95
    INMED director 91, 94
    medical education 93–94
Stomach Tea 57
suffering, ritual 15
surgery 8
    death from 7
Swimmer xiii, **23-33**, *26*
    Cherokee healer 23
    death 32
    early education 24–25

T

Ta-boodle **1–11**
    origin of name 2–3
    as surgeon 7–8
    and White Horse 1
Ta-boodle's gravestone *10*
taboos, and disease treatment 31
Tap-to
    Ta-boodle's treatment 11
T'ebodal. *See* Ta-boodle
Tennessee 23
Texas Panhandle 3
The American Journal of Nursing 48
The Red Man 47–48
Thilgeyah (mother of Montezuma)
    35
Thomas, William H. 27
time
    Indian concept 13, 65

Tonto tribe (Apache) 45
Treaty of New Echota 24
tuberculosis 73
Tumoon, Mary (mother of Chief
    Two Moon Meridas) 52
Two Moon Herb Company 52
Tyler, Varro E. 57

U

University of Utah 66
Utah State Hospital 66
Ute 3
Ute Indian Reservation 66
Ute Mental Health Clinic 66

V

Vassar College 47
visions xi, 16, 17
vocables 108

W

Wadsworth, Clarence Raymond
    (husband of Ruth Hills
    Wadsworth) 48
Wadsworth, Ruth Hills **44-50**
    adoption 46
    birth 45
    death 50
    in France 49
    marriage to Clarence 48

nursing career 44–45
nursing education 47
return to Mescalero tribe 49
Wahpeton tribe 62
Washington 39
Washita River 4
Wassaja. *See* Montezuma
Wassaja (Montezuma's newspa-
    per) *41*, 42
water monster spirit 5
whales 69
Whitecloud Center 66
white medicine xiii, 6, 20, 23, 31
    and Indian medicine 27–29
white sage 16
white traders 5
Wichita Mountains 105
willow bark xiii
Winnebago tribe 112
World Health Organization 82
World War I 44
Wounded Knee, Battle of 62
Wyoming 2
Wyoming State Hospital 66

Y

Yavapai tribe 35, 40
    and Montezuma's death 43
Yellowstone River 2
Yuit tribe 70